Ten Commandments

10 Commandments

The Secrets of Spiritual Growth Found in God's Principles for Living

EMANUEL SWEDENBORG

Translated by
B. Erikson Odhner, Jonathan S. Rose,
and George F. Dole

Edited by
Morgan Beard

Swedenborg
Foundation

West Chester, Pennsylvania

Library of Congress Cataloging-in-Publication Data

Names: Swedenborg, Emanuel, 1688–1772, author. | Odhner, B. Erikson, translator. | Rose, Jonathan S., 1956– translator | Dole, George F., translator | Beard, Morgan, editor.

Title: Ten Commandments : the secrets of spiritual growth found in God's principles for living / Emanuel Swedenborg ; translated by B. Erikson Odhner, Jonathan S. Rose, and George F. Dole ; edited by Morgan Beard.

Description: West Chester, Pennsylvania : Swedenborg Foundation, 2016.

Identifiers: LCCN 2016033639 (print) | LCCN 2016038323 (ebook) | ISBN 9780877854319 (alk. paper) | ISBN 9780877856955

Subjects: LCSH: New Jerusalem Church--Doctrines.

Classification: LCC BX8711.A7 B433 2016 (print) | LCC BX8711.A7 (ebook) | DDC 230/.94--dc23

LC record available at https://lccn.loc.gov/2016033639

Edited by John Connolly

Design and typesetting by Karen Connor

"*Revelation Explained* (1758–59)" and "*Secrets of Heaven* (1754)" were translated by B. Erikson Odhner.

"*Life* (1763)" was originally published in Emanuel Swedenborg, *Life / Faith,* trans. George F. Dole (West Chester, PA: Swedenborg Foundation, 2014).

"*True Christianity* (1771)" was originally published as "The Catechism, or Ten Commandments, Explained in Both Its Outer and Its Inner Meanings," in Emanuel Swedenborg, *True Christianity*, vol. 1, trans. Jonathan S. Rose (West Chester, PA: Swedenborg Foundation, 2006).

In many places throughout the manuscript, the scripture quotations reflect the translators' rendering of Swedenborg's original Latin in order to maintain consistency with Swedenborg's commentary. Where this was not necessary, scripture quotations are taken from the New Revised Standard Version Bible, copyright © 1989 by the Division of Christian Education of the National Council of the Churches of Christ in the USA, and are used by permission. All rights reserved.

Printed in the United States of America

Swedenborg Foundation
320 North Church Street
West Chester, PA 19380
www.swedenborg.com

Contents

≒

—◇—

—◆—

True Christianity (1771)

Introduction

⇌

Several years ago, I had the opportunity to teach a course on Christian ethics to maximum-security prisoners. This course was part of a program sponsored by Mercer University that was designed to give inmates an opportunity to work toward a college degree—even while they were serving time in prison. The courses were taught at the Clyde N. Phillips State Prison in Buford, Georgia, and those who completed the program received a bachelor of science degree in human resources management.

As I began the course, I told the story from the Gospels about the rich, young ruler who had come to Jesus saying, "Teacher, what good thing shall I do that I may have eternal life?" (Matthew 19:16). I went on to explain that Jesus said, "Why do you call me good? No one is good but One, that is, God. But if you want to enter into life . . ."

I paused, letting the unfinished sentence hang in the air.

During the pause, I looked around at the class of thirty men, all wearing their prison uniforms (white shirts and white pants with blue stripes on the side). They were quiet, polite, and seemingly interested. I repeated the sentence again. "*If you want to enter into life . . .*" And then I asked, "How did Jesus finish that sentence? What did Jesus say?"

Several students raised their hands to answer the question. I wasn't surprised. After all, this prison was in the heart of the Bible Belt, and most of these men had Baptist backgrounds. The first student to respond said, "Sell what you have and give to the poor." Around the classroom, heads were nodding in agreement. The case seemed settled. To all appearances, my students had passed their first test.

"That's a good answer," I said. "Jesus did say that a few verses later. But that was not the first thing he said. Does anyone know what Jesus said first?" The class was quiet. No one seemed to know, or if someone did know, he was not offering an answer.

So I told them: "Jesus said, 'If you want to enter into life, *keep the commandments*'" (Matthew 19: 17). I then explained that since this was going to be a course about Christian ethics, our focus was going to be on the Ten Commandments. After all, what could be more important as a foundation for Christian life than knowing the Ten Commandments? In fact, I explained, the Ten Commandments have long been considered the foundation for ALL ethical systems—not just for Christianity.

Not all the men in class were Christians. Some were Muslim, a few were Buddhist or Jewish, and many had no religious affiliation at all. But all of them seemed to accept that the Ten Commandments were a universal ethical code. Quoting Kahlil Gibran's "A Poet's Voice," I told them that "the varied paths of religion are but the fingers of the loving hand of the Supreme Being, extended to all." And I introduced them to the teachings of Swedish philosopher and visionary Emanuel Swedenborg (1688–1772), beginning with his statement, "In every religion there are laws like those of the Ten Commandments . . . [and] we are saved by living according to these laws" (*Divine Providence* 254:2).

This, of course, is very different from the idea that only Christians can be saved or that Christ's death on the cross did away with the need to keep the Ten Commandments. The radical idea that everyone can be saved as long as they live according to the Ten Commandments seemed to be accepted without protest. In fact, I had the feeling that a wave of relief rippled through the room as this simple yet profound truth was expressed.

Over the ten weeks that followed, I taught my students not only about the literal sense of the commandments but also about their deeper levels. For example, the deeper level of the commandment against murder made intuitive sense to them. While many had firsthand experience with the literal level of this commandment, they clearly understood that being angry at someone or calling a person "worthless" is also a form of murder. One of them told me that his cellmate had "stabbed him in the back"—not physically but in the sense that the individual had said destructive things about him.

When we discussed the sixth commandment, they understood that there was more to adultery than the physical act, as Jesus had said that "everyone who looks at a woman with lust has already committed adultery with her in his heart" (Matthew 5:28).

It was a good course. There were many, many stories about breakthroughs in spiritual development that had come from simply striving to keep the commandments. There was much laughter, there were tears, there were new friendships, and there were many occasions of spontaneous applause, as these "stars in stripes" rose above the promptings of their lower nature to live according to the commandments. It felt like heaven on earth. These fine men were still in prison, but they were *entering life*.

Years later, as this book was being prepared, one of those men wrote to me about how his perspective on the Ten Commandments had changed:

I had been raised in a strict religious environment and was taught a very rigid view of the commandments. Being forced to follow every commandment to the letter placed an impossible burden on me. The commandments were presented, not as stepping stones inviting me into a relationship with God, but rather as sledgehammers to beat me down. The atmosphere of religious rigidity was too much for me—I felt so stifled that I could not breathe.

To make matters worse, I was the victim of religious hatred and persecution. We were the only Catholic family in a Southern Baptist neighborhood. Back in those days, prejudice against Catholics was as strong as bigotry against blacks. It's something I never understood and still don't to this day.

As a result, I just didn't care about religion anymore. Since it was impossible to keep the commandments, why try? How can anyone do the impossible? And if religion is about bigotry and prejudice, who needs it? This, of course, led to rebellion. As I descended into darker and darker places, I sinned in every way imaginable and may have even invented some new ones! In brief, beginning at as early as twelve years old, I broke into a run on the path of self-destruction, and I didn't look back until I ran into the wall of incarceration.

As a maximum security prisoner, I was given the job of law clerk in the prison library. My job was to sort through the hundreds of donated books and arrange them appropriately. It was there, among those books, that I found a pearl: *Divine Love and Wisdom* by Emanuel Swedenborg. After reading only a few pages, I sensed that there was something truly special about this book, even though the language was hard to understand. Nevertheless, those three words of the title,

"Love" "And" "Wisdom," seemed to say it all: **LAW**—the Divine Law.

And so I prayed that God would send someone to help me understand the words and insights of this book. The answer to this prayer from a soul in hell came in the form of a Mercer University course called "Christian Ethics."

You began by asking us what Jesus said when he was asked, "What good thing should be done in order to have eternal life?" I was among those who said, "Sell what you have and give to the poor." But you pointed out that Jesus did not begin with those words. Instead, he began by saying, "If you want to enter into life, keep the commandments." I now see that this is a necessary beginning—it's how we enter into life. In doing so, we eventually come to the realization that we cannot do it without God's power. That's when we realize that it's not so much about entering into life as it is about allowing Life to enter into us.

Vin Deloria Jr., the Sioux Indian, put it well when he said, "Religion is for those who are afraid of going to hell. Spirituality is for those who have already been there." I was in hell, and God came to me through the Ten Commandments.

From time to time, many of us find ourselves in a kind of prison. It might be an anxious thought that keeps coming back again and again. It might be an old resentment or a persistent complaint that will not go away. Even though we may try to temporarily distract ourselves with work; amuse ourselves with entertainment; or drown our emotions in alcohol, drugs, or destructive relationships, it is always there, ready to remind us that we are still in captivity. We cannot shake it off, let it go, or rise above it. It is a kind of emotional and spiritual imprisonment. In religious terms, this kind of bondage is called "hell," and as our Sioux friend reminds us, many of us have been there.

The Ten Commandments are a divinely given curriculum for breaking free of the negativity that binds us. This promise is made clear in their opening words: "I am the Lord your God, who brought you out of the land of Egypt, *out of the house of bondage*" (Exodus 20:2). The God who gave us the Ten Commandments is the same God who came to earth to tell us that "the truth will make you free" (John 8:32).

Learning the commandments and keeping them at the literal level is a good start. We have indeed found the key to the prison door, and we are on our way to freedom. Nevertheless, we have just begun to *enter into* life. If we choose to continue, then for the rest of our lives and throughout all eternity we will be keeping the commandments at deeper and deeper levels. As Swedenborg says, "It is important to realize that the principles of the Ten Commandments are intended as rules both for those in this world and those in heaven" (*Secrets of Heaven* 8899).

This is why Swedenborg's work is so significant. It was his belief that the Word of God contained infinite depths of meaning. According to Swedenborg, there is first of all the literal, or *earthly*, sense that is primarily about the world of time and space—our physical actions. Within the literal sense is a deeper *spiritual* sense, which deals with our inner world of thoughts and feelings, especially in regard to our neighbor. And then within both the earthly and spiritual senses is an inmost, or *heavenly*, sense, which deals exclusively with our relationship to God. As we progress in our spiritual development, the Lord reveals to us the deeper truths that we need as we continue to enter into life—a life of ever-increasing love, wisdom, and useful service.

From the time of his first spiritual awakening until his death at the age of eighty-two, Swedenborg devoted himself to the publication of twenty-five Latin volumes that describe the earthly, spiritual, and heavenly senses of sacred scripture

(among many other topics). In three of his major works—
Secrets of Heaven (1749–56), *Revelation Explained* (unpublished
during his lifetime but written during 1758 and 1759), and *True
Christianity* (1771)—he carefully explains how the Ten Commandments contain each of these senses. He also has a discussion of several of the commandments and how they relate
to spiritual growth in his short work *Life* (1763). While the
exposition of the commandments in each book contains the
same fundamental message, the three treatments amplify,
augment, and enhance each other in wonderful ways. Key
details that are omitted or barely mentioned in one book are
explained in greater depth in the other books. These differ-
ences supplement each other beautifully, helping us reach
levels of insight that could not be attained by reading only
one of the treatments.

It should also be mentioned that Swedenborg follows the
traditional ordering of the commandments as practiced in the
Lutheran tradition. This means that he treats as a single commandment (the first commandment) the prohibition against
having other gods and worshipping idols; he also treats the
two parts of the commandment against coveting as the ninth
and tenth commandments. He reads the words "You shall not
covet your neighbor's house" as a commandment against the
inordinate desire to possess the things of the world (our tendency to be materialistic); and he reads the words "You shall
not covet your neighbor's wife, or male or female slave, or ox,
or donkey" as a commandment against our inordinate desire
to rule over others (our tendency to be controlling). It is inter-
esting that the Bible never refers to the commandments by
number—perhaps because it's vastly more important to *keep
the commandments* than it is to number them.

In Swedenborg's day, many sincere Christians believed that
since they were saved by a faith in Christ's vicarious atone-
ment, the commandments were no longer necessary. The idea

that "faith is all you need" was, for many, the essence of spirituality. But Swedenborg was adamant that this view was misguided. He believed that Jesus's statement "If you love me, you will keep my commandments" (John 14:15) refers to more than the two great and most general commandments—love the Lord, and love your neighbor. More specifically, Jesus was referring to the first tablet of the Ten Commandments, which teaches us how to love the Lord, and to the second tablet of the Ten Commandments, which teaches us how to love our neighbor. For Swedenborg, then, the Ten Commandments teach us *how to love*:

> Loving the Lord means love and passion for doing what he enjoins us to do, namely, keep his commandments. To the extent we obey or keep these commandments with love and passion, we are loving the Lord, because they are the Lord's presence with us. (*Revelation Explained* 981)

Swedenborg describes what happens within the soul of a person who strives to keep the commandments, especially one who has the realization that these are not just civil and moral teachings but are divinely given laws of religion:

> Obeying the commandments purifies our inner being, opens up heaven, and allows the Lord to come in. With respect to our spirit it makes us an angel of heaven. (*Revelation Explained* 902:6)

It is true that most of the Ten Commandments are prohibitions in the form of "You shall not," and this phrasing may seem to be in direct contrast with their positive, life-affirming purpose. Swedenborg explains that the commandments are written this way because the first step in spiritual growth is to abstain from evil:

> In the preceding article on "works" we said that our own endeavors are not good works; the only good works are those

accomplished by the Lord when he is present with us. But two things are necessary in order for our endeavors to be accomplished by the Lord and not by us. First, we must recognize the Lord's divine nature, acknowledging him as the God of heaven and earth even with respect to his human manifestation, and we must realize that anything good that happens is done by him. Secondly, we must live according to the Ten Commandments, abstaining from the evil behavior that is forbidden by them: worshipping other gods, profaning the name of God, stealing, committing adultery, murdering, giving false testimony, and craving the possessions and property belonging to other people.

These are the two prerequisites for our endeavors to be good, because everything good comes from the Lord, and because he cannot enter us and lead us unless or until that wicked behavior has been removed as a sin. That behavior is hellish—in fact, it is hell within us—and until hell is removed the Lord cannot come in and open up heaven. (*Revelation Explained* 934:2)

This may explain why the time I spent in prison teaching the Ten Commandments was "heaven on earth" for me. Through the honest acknowledgment of past and present sins and our striving to avoid them in the future, heaven was opened and God was present. We felt a new hope—even within those cement walls—for we knew that the Lord was leading us out of the house of bondage and into heavenly freedom.

May this be your experience as well as you read the pages of this book.

RAY SILVERMAN
Meadowbrook, PA

—◇—

Editor's Note

For Emanuel Swedenborg (1688–1772), the Ten Commandments were an integral part of spiritual living. They provided a list of evil actions to be avoided—or good actions to be embraced—that formed the key to regeneration, the process of spiritual rebirth. Just as Swedenborg found a deeper meaning encased within the literal text of the Bible, he perceived a deeper spiritual teaching within the simple instructions in the Ten Commandments. Scattered throughout his published and unpublished theological works are four extended commentaries on that inner meaning, now published here in a single volume for the first time.

Swedenborg's earliest discussion of the Ten Commandments occurs in *Secrets of Heaven* (also known by its Latin title, *Arcana Coelestia*). This multivolume magnum opus, considered by many to be the first of his published theological works, is a verse-by-verse exegesis of the inner meaning of the biblical books of Genesis and Exodus. The discussion of the Ten Commandments occurs naturally as part of Swedenborg's commentary on Exodus 20, which appears in volume 7 of the original Latin edition (1754). While that portion of the text is effectively a sustained discussion of the Ten Commandments, Swedenborg focuses on the spiritual correspondence of the words in each verse and structures his commentary according to the content of individual verses rather than to their division by commandment. (In this volume, the subheadings connecting the verses to their respective commandments were inserted by the editor to aid the reader in locating and comparing Swedenborg's discussion of specific commandments.)

Swedenborg first addresses the Ten Commandments as a separate, self-contained topic in *Revelation Explained* (Latin *Apocalypsis Explicata*, also known in English as *Apocalypse Explained*). This verse-by-verse commentary on the book of Revelation was never completed within Swedenborg's lifetime; it was discovered and published after his death. Based on references within the text to Swedenborg's previously published works and an expected date of publication in one of the drafts, it was likely written during 1758 and 1759. As is done in *Secrets of Heaven*, interspersed between the biblical commentary in *Revelation Explained* are essays on various spiritual topics, and the *Revelation Explained* material in this volume is one of those essays.

Swedenborg's next published commentary on the Ten Commandments occurs in his 1763 short work *Life* (Latin *Doctrina Vitae*), traditionally known as *The Doctrine of Life* and often published with three other short works of the same year under the title *The Four Doctrines*. Broadly speaking, *Life* is about spiritual growth, and the bulk of this short work is taken up by a discussion of the Ten Commandments, although not every commandment is addressed directly.

Swedenborg's final commentary on the Ten Commandments occurs in his 1771 *True Christianity* (Latin *Vera Christiana Religio*, also known in English as *True Christian Religion*). The last of Swedenborg's published theological works, *True Christianity* is structured as a series of chapters on various doctrinal topics, of which the Ten Commandments is one. This is Swedenborg's most concise full commentary on the Ten Commandments.

Although there are overlaps in content between these texts—in some places, the similarities are so strong that it suggests Swedenborg may have copied from earlier sources in writing later volumes—each commentary has unique features that complement the others.

Swedenborg's Numbering of the Commandments and Biblical Citation. The most commonly cited version of the Ten Commandments occurs in Exodus 20:1–17 in most editions of the Bible (there is another version in Deuteronomy 5:4–21). In *Secrets of Heaven*, however, Swedenborg follows Sebastian Schmidt's 1696 Latin edition of the Bible, in which the same text is divided into only fourteen verses.

The commandments are not numbered in the Bible; and in fact, the verses that list the commandments contain more than ten imperatives. Different faith traditions divide the commandments in various ways. Raised as part of a devout Lutheran family, Swedenborg follows the traditional Lutheran division of the commandments.

In *Revelation Explained*, Swedenborg reverses the traditional order of two of the commandments, listing the prohibition against theft as the fifth commandment and the injunction against murder as the seventh (retaining adultery as the sixth). In his other theological works, he keeps to the usual order. Swedenborg does not comment on why he made the reversal in *Revelation Explained*, but it may have simply been a mistake. A critical note to a translation by John C. Ager (*Apocalypse Explained*, West Chester, PA: Swedenborg Foundation, 1994–97) suggests that Swedenborg was following the verse order given in the Septuagint, a Greek translation of the Hebrew Bible. While it is possible that Swedenborg had been informed by the ordering in the Septuagint, the two versions are not a precise match (the Septuagint has the prohibition against adultery as the fifth commandment, then theft as the sixth and murder as the seventh).

Swedenborg assumes that readers are familiar with the text of the Bible and will sometimes offer commentary on specific words or phrases within a verse (or a commandment) without citing the verse explicitly. In case of confusion, the reader is encouraged to consult the biblical text of the commandment in question.

Section and Subsection Numbers. Following a practice that was common in his time, Swedenborg divided his published theological works into sections numbered in sequence from beginning to end. In this volume, his original section numbers are preserved as **bolded** numbers at the beginning of a paragraph. Because many sections throughout Swedenborg's works are too long for precise cross-referencing, Swedenborgian scholar John Faulkner Potts (1838–1923) further divided them into subsections; these have since become standard, although minor variations occur from one edition to another. In this volume, these subsections are indicated by bracketed numbers that appear within a section: [2], [3], and so on.

As is common in Swedenborgian studies, text citations of his works refer not to page numbers but to section numbers, which are uniform in most editions. In citations, the section symbol (§) is generally omitted when the section number reference is preceded by the title of a work by Swedenborg. Thus, "*Heaven and Hell* 239" would refer to section 239 of Swedenborg's *Heaven and Hell*, not to page 239 of any edition of that book. Subsection numbers are given after a colon; a reference such as "239:2" indicates subsection 2 of section 239.

Alterations to the Original Text. Swedenborg frequently provides extensive biblical references to support a point or cross-references to other places in his writings where he discusses similar points. For the sake of brevity, some of these lists have been shortened in this volume, and in some places (particularly in *Secrets of Heaven*) the cross-references have been omitted entirely. Places where text was removed are indicated with ellipses. In paragraphs with so many cross-references that the use of ellipses was judged to be disruptive, the cross-references were taken out without indication of their removal. In other instances, cross-references were edited to indicate their relationship to the text in this volume rather than to the original (for example, omitting a reference to text "above" or "below" where this volume does not include the referenced text). Readers who would like the benefit of the full list of references are encouraged to consult an edition of the relevant complete work.

In the excerpt from *Revelation Explained*, Swedenborg's biblical commentary was taken out so that the Ten Commandments material could be read as a continuous piece. The gaps where the commentary on Revelation would have appeared are represented in this volume by the symbol ⚜ ⚜ ⚜.

Harmonization of Terms. The texts in this volume were taken from different translations, and in some cases the translation of particular terms was harmonized for the sake of consistency. One example of this is the Latin *affectio*, which is commonly translated as *affection* but may also be rendered *feeling, desire, love, inclination toward*, or *response to*. In this volume, *affectio* appears as *passion*. Another harmonized term is the Latin *charitas*, which is generally translated as *charity* but can also appear as *caring*. Here, it is rendered *goodwill*.

One term that was *not* harmonized was the Latin *intellectus*, which Swedenborg often pairs with the Latin *voluntas* when describing two fundamental parts of our mind. *Intellectus* and *voluntas* are commonly translated *understanding* and *will*, respectively. Some of the text in this volume retains that usage; in other passages, *intellectus* is rendered *intellect*.

—◇—

Ten Commandments

Secrets of Heaven (1754)

Summary [of the Inner Meaning of Exodus 20:1–14]

8859. The inner meaning of this chapter deals with divine truths that must be implanted into the goodness of those who belong to the Lord's spiritual church. These truths are the Ten Commandments. . . .

Verse 1: And God Spoke All These Words

8860. *And God spoke all these words, saying* is symbolic of the fact that divine truth is provided to those in the heavens and on earth.

8861. This symbolic meaning is consistent with the fact that *the words God spoke* means the divine truth, since whatever God speaks is nothing but the truth. This is why in John 1:1 the divine truth is called *the Word* and why it says the Word is the Lord. The Lord was divine truth itself when he was in this world; and thereafter, when he was glorified, he became divine goodness. Ever since, divine truth has come entirely from him; and for the angels, this divine truth is their light. This light is, in fact, what illuminates our inner sight or our ability to understand.

[2] Because our inner sight sees spiritual and not worldly things, its focus is on truth. Its intellectual focus is on spiritual truth, which we call matters of faith. Its worldly focus is on the principles of civil affairs, which are concerned with being just, and also on the principles of morality, which are concerned with being honorable. Lastly, our inner sight focuses on earthly truth that is deduced from the objects of our physical senses, primarily the sense of sight.

We can see from this the order through which truth comes to us. It all originates in divine truth, which is the inner foundation of all truth. The outward forms within which we find this inner foundational truth likewise originate in divine truth, since they are created to receive and hold that truth. We can therefore infer that the phrase *all things were created by the Word* (John 1:1–3) means that divine truth is the absolute essence and the sole substance from which all truth comes.

8862. The words God spoke are divine truth being offered to those in the heavens and to those on earth, because these ten principles we call the Ten Commandments and the regulations that follow are truth that is suitable not only for those on earth but also for those in heaven, having been declared and commanded from Mt. Sinai. Every word (that is, every truth) spoken by the Lord is intended not only for humans but also for angels, reaching earth by passing through the heavens.

In the heavens, these truths do not sound the way they do on earth, because in the heavens, they are in a spiritual form instead of an earthly form. What the spiritual form is like compared with its earthly form becomes obvious when we consider both the inner and the literal meanings of everything mentioned in the Word: the inner meanings are spiritual, but the literal meanings are earthly—the latter being accommodated to those on earth and the former accommodated to those in the heavens.

[2] This makes sense because the Word has actually been sent from a divine origin, passing through the heavens until reaching earth. When it arrives on earth, truth is accommodated to the human race, which has an earthly and materialistic focus. In the heavens, it is accommodated to angels, who focus on what is spiritual and heavenly. As such, the Word is sacred in its own right, since it contains what is heavenly and divine.

The principles of the Ten Commandments are certain proof of this. Everyone is capable of knowing these commandments, such as they are known all over the world: that we should honor our parents, should not commit murder, should not commit adultery, should not steal, and should not give false testimony. The Israelite nation was able to know these commandments, and they viewed things purely from a worldly perspective. Is there any nation that does not know them? Nonetheless, to ensure their dissemination, Jehovah himself descended and proclaimed them in a fire whose flames reached the very heart of heaven. It is obvious that these principles involve a lot more at their core than appears on the surface, namely, truth that is just as relevant to the heavens and that fills the heavens.

Everything in the Word is of this nature, because it comes from a divine source. This explains why the Word is holy, being referred to as *inspired in every jot and every little stroke* (Matthew 5:18; Luke 16:17).

In the following sections, you will see what the principles of the Ten Commandments are like in their spiritual meaning, that is, as they appear in the heavens.

Verses 2–6: You Shall Not Have Other Gods before My Face

8863. *I am Jehovah your God, who led you out of the land of Egypt, out of the house of slaves. You shall not have other* *gods before my face. You shall not make for yourself a carved image or any likeness of anything that is in the heavens above or that is in the earth beneath or that is in the waters under the earth. You shall not bow down to them or serve them, because I am Jehovah your God, God the Zealous, bringing the consequences of the fathers' wickedness on the sons, on the third generation and on the fourth generation among those who hate me; and performing mercy to thousands among those who love me and keep my commandments. You shall not utter the name of Jehovah your God unworthily, because Jehovah will not render innocent the person who utters his name unworthily.*

8864. *I am Jehovah your God* symbolizes the Lord's deified human manifestation as universally sovereign over every single thing that relates to goodness and truth. This is obvious from the fact that in the Word *Jehovah* means none other than the Lord. The same is true of *Jehovah Zebaoth, the Lord Jehovih, and Jehovah God.*

The Lord is called *Jehovah* in reference to his divine goodness, which is what essentially makes him divine; but he is called *God* in reference to his divine truth, which is his divine nature in action. *Jehovah God* means the Lord's deified human manifestation, because this aspect of the Lord is referred to in the Word by both *Jehovah* and *God. Jehovah* means divine goodness, which also defines him in terms of his human aspect; and *God* means the divine truth, which is what comes forth from him.

[2] *Jehovah God* refers to the Lord's deified human manifestation, because in the heavens they cannot picture or even sense the divinity that is actually within the Lord and therefore cannot believe in it or love it. They can only picture and sense a deified human being.

The concept of God being divine cannot actually be communicated to the angels in heaven, let alone to humans on earth, except through the idea of a deified human being. This is generally acknowledged in our churches because of the Lord's words in the Gospels, in which he says that *he is the door*, that *he is the intermediary*, that *no one can approach the Father except through him*, that *no one other than him knows the Father*, and that *no one has seen the Father, not even a glimpse of him*. Obviously, it is the Lord who is referred to here by *Jehovah God*.

It is also generally acknowledged that it is the Lord himself who has redeemed the human race and saved it from hell, as symbolized in the next phrase: *I led you out of the land of Egypt, out of the house of slaves*. This proves that Jehovah God, who spoke from Mount Sinai, is the Lord as a deified human being.

[3] This is the first thing said by the Lord from Mount Sinai, because it must be universally sovereign in each and every idea that follows. Whatever is said first must be kept in mind in what follows it and should be seen as the universal principle contained within it. We will see in the next section what *universally sovereign* means.

The words spoken by the Lord are no exception. Whatever he said first must govern what follows, incorporating not only what was said first but everything after that. What follows in chapter 20 [of Exodus] are the principles of the Ten Commandments, which are inner truths, followed by the regulations, which are outward truths. Within these inner and outward truths, the Lord must govern as a deified human being, as he is their source and their essence. To be sure, genuine truth comes entirely from him, and he *is* whatever comes from him.

It is also widely recognized in our churches that the Lord as a deified human being governs every aspect of faith. We are taught that without the Lord there is no salvation and that everything good and true in our faith comes from him.

As he is the source of faith, he *is* faith. And if he is faith, he is also every truth contained in the teachings about faith that are found in the Word. This is also why the Lord is called *the Word*.

[4] As I said before, ideas that come first must govern the ideas that come next and therefore the whole sequence. This is demonstrated by each and every thing the Lord spoke, especially the prayer that we know as the Lord's Prayer. Every idea in that prayer follows in a sequence, like a pillar that gets wider from the top toward the base. At the center of this pillar are the primary truths in the sequence. The principal truth is on the very inside, and each idea that follows in the sequence is gradually added to it; and in this way, the pillar grows. This innermost truth is universally sovereign within all of the truths surrounding it, because it essentially sustains them all.

8865. The comments and illustrations in *Secrets of Heaven* 8853–58 clarify what *universally sovereign* means. For humans, what is universally sovereign is that which can be found within every single one of our thoughts and wishes. It is therefore what constitutes our very mind and life. The Lord must be our sovereign, because it is so for the angels in heaven, of whom we say *they are in the Lord*.

The Lord becomes our sovereign when we not only trust that all goodness and truth are given to us by him but also when we love the fact that this is so. The angels not only trust that this is the case but also have an awareness of it. This is why their life is the Lord's life within them. Their life's desire is to live in the love given to them by the Lord, and their life's understanding consists in living in the faith given to them by the Lord.

This explains why the Lord is the all in all of heaven and why he himself *is* heaven. When the Lord is sovereign within us, the members of his church, as universally as he is within the angels of heaven, then he is within everything we believe to be good and true. This is like the heart's relationship to every blood vessel, because blood vessels originate in the heart and draw from it the blood for which they exist.

[2] We should recognize that the kind of spirits or angels who are around us depends on what is universally sovereign within us. This is because within each one of us, what is universally sovereign is the essence of our life (*Secrets of Heaven* 8853, 8858). We are perfectly cheerful and content even when we are thinking about other things, because the angels and spirits around us live within this sovereignty as though they are living in the same house with us, and their happiness flows into us and causes this cheerful and content feeling.

People are not aware that this is where their happiness comes from. They do not know that their life flows into them or that what is universally sovereign in them constitutes their very life. Neither do they know that when what is sovereign in their life is being stimulated, it is like the pupil in the eye making contact with an object it sees: people experience pleasure when the eye sees beautiful objects and displeasure when it sees ugly objects.

We call something universal when it embraces every aspect, and so what is universally sovereign in us is what is in each and every part of us.

8866. *Who led you out of the land of Egypt, out of the house of slaves.* This symbolizes being freed from hell by the Lord, as is obvious from the symbolism of *to lead out of* as being liberation, from the symbolism of *the land of Egypt* as being assaulted by hellish spirits, and also from the symbolism of *the house of slaves* as being spiritual captivity. *The house of slaves* means spiritual captivity and also hell, because being a slave means being held captive and led by those who are in hell. Being free means being led by the Lord. Those who belong to the spiritual church, represented by the sons of Israel, have been freed from hell by the Lord.

8867. *You shall not have other gods before my face.* The symbolism of this is that we are not to think truth comes from any source other than the Lord. This is because *gods* is symbolic of what is true and in the negative sense of what is false; and *face*—when speaking of God—is symbolic of love, mercy, peace, goodness, and therefore the Lord himself, since these things come from him.

Another reason *you shall not have other gods before my face* symbolizes that we are not to think truth comes from any source other than the Lord is because the Lord's deified human manifestation, symbolized by *I am Jehovah your God*, is the first thing mentioned. Therefore, it is the first in the sequence and must be universally sovereign within every single truth that follows.

And now are established the kinds of things we must avoid because they would ruin or prevent the Lord from being universally sovereign within each and every truth contained in the principles and laws declared and commanded from Mount Sinai. The main thing that would prevent this from happening is to think truth comes from some source other than the Lord, symbolized by *you shall not have other gods before my face.*

The other things that would prevent this universal sovereignty from happening are the things that follow in the sequence: that they should not make graven images for themselves; should make no likenesses of the things that are in the heavens, in the earth, and in the waters; and should not bow down to them or serve them. After these are specified, *because I am Jehovah your God* is repeated as a symbol that the Lord must be within each and every truth.

8868. We should also say something briefly about truth that comes from somewhere other than the Lord. Generally speaking, this is truth that does not have the Lord within it. Truth does not have the Lord within it any time we deny him and his divinity or likewise when we acknowledge him but still arrogate to ourselves his righteousness, believing goodness and truth are not given to us by him but that they come from ourselves.

Truth does not have the Lord within it when we take it from the Word (especially in its literal meaning) and use it to argue in favor of our control over other people or for our own enrichment. Because it comes from the Word, this is actually truth; it is not true here, though, because it is used in arguing for a sinister purpose and therefore is perverted. This is the kind of thing that is meant by the Lord's words in Matthew,

> If anyone says to you, "Look! Here is the Messiah!" or "There he is"— do not believe it. For false messiahs and false prophets will appear and produce great signs and omens, to lead astray, if possible, even the elect. (Matthew 24:23–24)

See also *Secrets of Heaven* 3900, and this in Luke,

> Beware that you are not led astray; for many will come in my name and say, "I am he!" and "The time is near!" Do not go after them. (Luke 21:8)

[2] Truth that comes from the Lord always remains the Lord's truth because of its inner aspect. Truth that does not come from the Lord appears to be true only from its outward appearance. It is not true in its inner aspect, because within it is vanity, falsity, and evil.

For something to be true, there needs to be life in it; and truth without life is truth we do not believe. Life does not come from anywhere other than being good, that is, through goodness that is given to us by the Lord. If the Lord is not within the truth, it is truth without life and therefore not truth. But if there is falsity or wickedness within our truth, then that truth is actually falsity and wickedness. It is what is inside that matters, and in the other life this shines through the outward appearance.

From this, we should understand what it means not to think of truth as coming from anywhere other than the Lord.

[3] Since few people understand this concept of truth being true in its inner aspect (and therefore being made into living truth by the Lord), I will say something about it based on my experience. In the other life, they understand what lies behind a person's words, for example, whether the person is concealing something or is being open about it. They also sense a person's intention: if the intention is good, they feel a gentleness within the words, but if the motivation is evil, they sense a harshness within the words, and so forth.

Speech among the angels in heaven is entirely transparent, to the point that the Lord's presence can be felt within it. The angels sense his presence unmistakably, and they even hear his presence in the gentleness of the speech and the way it sounds.

This also makes it possible in the other life to learn what lies within truth and whether the Lord is within it or not. Truth in which the Lord resides is living truth, but truth in which the Lord does not reside is not living truth. Living truth is truth that we believe because we love the Lord and are kind to other people. Truth that is not alive is not true, because within it lies self-love and worldly ambition.

This transparency enables spirits and angels to discern whether the truth any of them speaks is consistent with how they live, or in other words, is consistent with what is universally sovereign within them.

8869. *You shall not make for yourself a carved image* is symbolic of not relying on our own intelligence. This makes sense, because a *carved image* is a symbol of something that does not come from the Lord but from our ego. A *carved image* symbolizes the product of our own intellect, and a *cast image* symbolizes our own desires. When we regard either the one or the other as our god and worship it, we love whatever comes from ourselves more than anything else.

People who do this actually do not believe that intelligence or wisdom flows into them from God. They attribute it all to themselves. Whatever happens to them they ascribe to luck or chance, and they flatly deny that divine providence has anything to do with it. They assume that if there is any external agency involved, it is in the order of nature, to which they attribute all things. To be sure, they publicly say some creator god has put his stamp on nature, yet in their heart they deny there is any god presiding over nature.

These are the kind of people who in their heart attribute everything to their own prudence and intelligence and attribute nothing to God. If they love themselves, they worship their own prudence and intelligence, and they expect other people to worship them as well. In fact, they would like to be worshipped as gods, if the church did not clearly forbid it. These are the fashioners of carved images, and their carved images are the ideas they carve out with their own egotism. They want those ideas to be worshipped as though they are divine.

[2] We can confirm that carved images in the Word are symbols of our own intelligence and our own desires by looking at many passages where they are mentioned, as in Jeremiah,

> Everyone becomes stupid and without knowledge, and the goldsmith is shamed by his carved image, because his cast image is a lie, and there is no spirit in those things. (Jeremiah 10:14, 51:17)

It says *everyone becomes stupid and without knowledge, and the goldsmith is shamed by his carved image* because *carved image* is symbolic of what comes not from the Lord but from our own intelligence. There is no spiritual life in what we carve out with our own intelligence. Spiritual life only comes from the Lord, and so the phrase *and there is no spirit in those things* is added.

[3] In Habakkuk,

> Because its maker has carved it, what value is the cast image?
> It is a cast image and a teacher of lies, for its maker trusts in
> what has been made, though the product is only an idol that
> cannot speak! . . . There is no spirit in it at all. (Habakkuk
> 2:18, 19)

Here, *carved image* is a symbol of the ideas we carve out with our own intelligence, in which there is no life from the Lord. . . .

8870. *Or any likeness* symbolizes an imitation of what comes from God, which is clear from the symbolism of *likeness* as being an imitation. What precedes this phrase and what follows it make clear that it means an imitation of what comes from God. It is preceded by *you shall have no other gods before my face* and *you shall not make for yourself a carved image.* This is symbolic of truth coming from some source other than God and yet still resembling the truth. It is followed by phrases like *that is in the heavens, that is on the earth,* and *that is in the waters.* These mean the kinds of things that come from a divine source, wherever they may be found.

[2] At this point, I should say what *an imitation of the things that come from a divine source* means, since we will be dealing with it in the rest of this verse and the beginning of the next. Imitating things that come from a divine source occurs when people profess divine thoughts in public and even perform

the sort of works commanded by God, thereby misleading others into believing that they are good and believe the truth when in fact they are thinking the exact opposite in their heart and wish nothing but evil. Such people are frauds, hypocrites, and deceivers. These are the people who *make an imitation of what comes from a divine source.*

In the other life, evil spirits *make an imitation of what comes from a divine source* when they create an outward mask or pretense, with nothing divine inside. This is practiced in the other life by frauds, hypocrites, deceivers, and in general everyone who from frequent practice develops the habit of speaking differently from the way they are thinking and of acting differently from the way they want to act. Some do this to boost their reputation so that they may fool people into thinking they are good. Some do it to have power.

[3] In the other life, any kind of mask or pretense constitutes a misuse of correspondences. The façade that enables them to feign goodwill and faith is gradually stripped away so that they are only acting from the actual nature they developed in the world and no longer acting with any pretense or hypocrisy.

Spirits of such a kind, realizing they are going to be deprived of this façade, claim that if they could be allowed to keep it, they would be able to get along with their friends and to seem to be doing good in the other life in the same way they had previously done in the world. Yet this cannot happen, because by means of this façade of seeming to do good they would be able to communicate in some fashion with heaven. Specifically, they would communicate with those on the outer fringes of heaven who are simple folk, equivalent to the skin on the human form of the macrocosm. Meanwhile, they would be communicating internally with the hells. The evil inside them predominates, because that is what they want; and the goodness of their feigned façade is only serving to acquire power on behalf of their evil impulses. Therefore, it is actually against the divine order of things to grant them license to act with guile and hypocrisy as they had in the world. These abilities are taken from them, and they are restored to the evil they truly want.

8871. *Of anything that is in the heavens above or that is on the earth beneath* is symbolic of seeing things with either spiritual or earthly enlightenment. The *likeness of anything that is in the heavens above* is symbolic of what appears in or is seen with spiritual enlightenment. These are all the considerations that relate to goodness and truth. They are matters of faith, of goodwill toward others, and of loving the Lord. Dissimulating or faking these is making a *likeness of anything that is in the heavens above.*

The *likeness of anything that is on the earth beneath* is symbolic of what appears in or is seen with earthly enlightenment. These are the sorts of considerations that are related to goodness and truth on a civil or moral level. Feigning or faking this is *making a likeness of anything that is on the earth beneath.*

The literal meaning of this phrase refers to what appears in the sky, like the sun, moon, and stars, or what appears on land, like different kinds of animals—flying, walking, and crawling. But the inner meaning of the phrase refers to the sorts of thing these symbols stand for, the things that relate to goodness and truth, as we said above.

[2] These considerations of goodness and truth are described in more detail in Moses:

> Do not act corruptly by making a carved image in the form of any figures—the likeness of male or female, the likeness of any animal that is on the earth, the likeness of any winged bird that flies in the air, the likeness of anything that creeps on the ground, the likeness of any fish that is in the water

under the earth. And when you look up to the heavens and see the sun, the moon, and the stars, all the host of heaven, do not be led astray and bow down to them and serve them. . . . Be careful not to forget the covenant that Jehovah your God made with you, and do not make for yourselves a carved image in the form of anything that Jehovah your God has forbidden you. For Jehovah your God is a devouring fire, a jealous God. . . . I call heaven and earth to witness against you today that you will soon utterly perish from the land . . . Jehovah will scatter you among the peoples; only a few of you will be left among the nations where Jehovah will lead you. There you will serve other gods made by human hands, objects of wood and stone that neither see, nor hear, nor eat, nor smell. (Deuteronomy 4:16–19, 23–28)

[3] The reason for such a severe prohibition against making a likeness of any object in the sky or on the earth is mainly that the nation descended from Jacob was strongly prone to worshipping the external aspect of things. They did not want to know anything about the inner life of the church—the things that relate to faith: loving the Lord and being kind to other people. If they had been allowed to make likenesses of things, they would have bowed down to them and worshipped them as gods. This is obvious from the golden calf they made for themselves despite so many miracles, and from their frequent lapses away from worshipping the deity and into idolatry. However, this is not what the inner meaning of these verses is talking about. It is talking about the concepts laid out above.

8872. *Or that is in the waters under the earth* is symbolic of what is on the plane of the physical and sensory. A *likeness of anything that is in the waters under the earth* is symbolic of what is below the things we see with our earthly enlightenment. It is obvious that these are things on the plane of the sensory and material when we consider the respective degrees of the human intellect. In the first degree is what we see with spiritual enlightenment, symbolized by something *that is in the heavens above*. In the second degree is what we see with earthly enlightenment, symbolized by something *that is on the earth beneath*. And in the third degree is what is on the plane of the sensory and material, symbolized by something *that is in the waters under the earth*.

Associated with this sensory and material plane are knowledge drawn largely from the evidence of the physical senses and our enjoyment of that knowledge. Such knowledge and its enjoyment are good things when put to good use by good people, but they are bad things when used for evil purposes by bad people. *Making a likeness of anything that is in the waters under the earth* means using this kind of knowledge to mislead others, as frauds, hypocrites, and deceivers are accustomed to do.

8873. *You shall not bow down to them or serve them* stands for not worshipping these imitations as divine. *Bowing down* is symbolic of humility, and *serving* is symbolic of submission. This refers to worshipping them as divine, because humility and submission are essential elements of worship. Without them, there is no worship—we are just going through the motions to imitate those elements of worship. There is no life in this gesture. Life from the Lord flows into a humble and submissive heart, because only such a heart is capable of receiving life. When the heart is truly humble, there is no self-love or worldly ambition to get in the way.

Two different terms are used because *bowing down* stands for worship that comes from loving what is good, and *serving* stands for worship that comes from believing what is true.

8874. *Because I am Jehovah your God* stands for divinity being in each and every word the Lord says, as is obvious from the explanations in §§8864 and 8865, above.

8875. *God the Zealous* symbolizes the fact that falsity and evil will result. The real meaning of *zealous God* is divine truth that comes from divine goodness. *God* is used in regard to truth, and *zealous* is used in regard to goodness, as will be seen below.

However, in relation to people who do not accept the divine truth that comes from the Lord's divine goodness, a *zealous God* means evil and falsity. Negative people see divine truth as falsity and see divine goodness as evil. It is viewed by each person according to that person's own character; and so the Lord's zeal, which is actually love and mercy, seems like anger to negative people.

When the Lord is protecting his own in heaven with love and mercy, those under the influence of evil get offended and angry at these good people. They rush into the zone that is influenced by divine truth and divine goodness in an attempt to destroy the people there. At that point, the divine truth that comes from divine goodness goes to work on them and causes them to feel torment similar to what is experienced in hell. This is why they attribute burning anger and indeed all evil to God, when in fact there is absolutely no anger and no evil in God, just pure forgiveness and mercy.

[2] It is obvious from these explanations why *zealous* stands for falsity and evil and why *zeal* stands for anger.

[3] The *Lord's zeal* is love and mercy, but when the Lord is protecting good people from evil people, it seems like hostility and even anger. This is demonstrated in the following passages in the Word, where the *Lord's zeal* is love and mercy.

In Isaiah,

Look down from heaven and see, from your holy and glorious habitation. Where is your zeal and your might? The yearning of your heart and your compassion? They are withheld from me. (Isaiah 63:15)

In this passage, *zeal* stands for mercy, which is a *yearning of the heart*, and refers to goodness. Where it says *your zeal and your might*, *zeal* refers to goodness, and *might* refers to truth. Likewise, *the yearning of your heart* refers to goodness, and *compassion* refers to truth; and in the same vein, *holy habitation* refers to the heaven where people from the celestial realm are, and *glorious habitation* refers to the heaven where people from the spiritual realm are. On account of heavenly marriage, which is the marriage between what is good and what is true, every time it talks about what is good in the Word, it also is talking about what is true. For example, the Lord is described with the twin names Jesus and Christ, which represents the divine marriage within the Lord. . . .

It is evident from these passages what *the zeal of Jehovah* or *a zealous God* means; the real meaning is love and mercy. But it seems like anger and devastation to those who are under the influence of evil and falsity, because they do not understand the real meaning.

[8] We should be aware that we particularly refer to Jehovah (that is, the Lord) as *jealous* or *vindictive* when our idea of what should be universally sovereign for someone in the church becomes corrupted. This is the idea that there is a deity and that we should love it, think about it, and revere it. When this idea is corrupted or destroyed, our enlightenment is replaced by a complete fog. There is no longer any divine influence on us, because we are not open to it; and this is why the commandment says *I am Jehovah your God, God the Zealous, bringing the consequences of the fathers' wickedness on the sons, on the third generation and on the fourth generation among those who hate me.*

This is what happens when we worship other gods or make for ourselves a carved image or any likeness. These things corrupt that concept of divinity, which is supposed to be universally sovereign.

[9] On this account, similar things are said elsewhere in Moses,

> Do not make for yourselves a carved image in the form of anything that Jehovah your God has forbidden you. For Jehovah your God is a devouring fire, a zealous God. (Deuteronomy 4:23, 24)

And also in Moses,

> You shall worship no other god, because Jehovah, whose name is Zealous, is a zealous God. (Exodus 34:14)

This was forbidden to the Israelite nation in such strong terms because the worship of other gods, of carved images, and of statues would completely destroy what represented the church among them. In heaven, Jehovah—that is, the Lord—is universally sovereign, and his divinity fills up everything there and makes everything alive. If that nation worshipped as divine anything other than the Lord, representation of the church would have completely perished and communication with heaven along with it.

8876. *Bringing the consequences of the fathers' wickedness on the sons* symbolizes falsity spreading as the result of the evil of idolatry. This is clear from the symbolism of *bringing the consequences of the fathers' wickedness* as the spread of evil. *Bringing [consequences]* refers to this spreading, because we are talking about the state of mind of those who completely reject the Lord's divinity. They are no longer receptive to goodness but only to evil, and this condition endures because the evil in such people constantly grows or spreads.

In a narrow sense, *bringing the consequences of the fathers' wickedness upon the sons* does not mean that sons will pay the price for their fathers' wickedness, which would be contrary to divine order (Deuteronomy 24:16). It means that the fathers' evil will grow; that this trait will be passed down to the children; and that in this way, evil accumulates progressively. The spiritual meaning, however, is not *fathers* but is *evil*, and it is not *sons* but is *falsity*. This is why these words symbolize the constant spread of falsity that results from evil.

8877. *On the third generation and on the fourth generation* symbolizes that there is a long progression of falsity and that it is connected. *Three* is the symbol of being complete from start to finish, meaning this is a long progression, and so *the third generation* is a long progression of falsity. *Four*, like *two*, is a symbol of being connected, and so *the third generation and the fourth generation* is a long progression of falsity that is connected.

We cannot help but find this interpretation of *the third generation and the fourth generation* strange or different from what the Word says; but we must remember that in the Word's inner meaning, numbers do not stand for numbers but stand for qualities.

8878. *Among those who hate me* stands for people who completely reject the Lord's divinity. This is consistent with the symbolism of *those who hate God* as being those who are under the influence of evil and the falsity that comes from evil. These are people who reject the Lord's divinity; and the more they are influenced by evil and the resulting falsity, the more they not only reject his divinity but also hate it.

It is the Lord's divine nature they are rejecting, because people who are under the influence of evil do not see with heavenly enlightenment. They see with earthly enlightenment and ultimately with the physical light they sense with their body, and in this light they can never see the Lord's human manifestation as being anything other than just human. They cannot understand what a deified human being is, because they have such an empty and meaningless concept of what *divine* means.

Suppose we put to them the following: The divine being is actually divine love, and divine love is the essence of all life.

From his conception, the Lord has been divine love—the innermost essence of life itself—and therefore he is Jehovah. He glorified his human manifestation into a likeness of Jehovah, which is to say, he made his human manifestation divine.

The ones with some intellectual ability can perhaps understand a certain amount of this, but still they do not believe it. When they fall out of the intellectual enlightenment that they temporarily enjoyed and come back into their own earthly or sensory enlightenment, they slip into a complete fog—and ultimately denial—regarding this truth.

8879. *And performing mercy to thousands* symbolizes that they will be permanently blessed with goodness and truth. This is consistent with the fact that *mercy* is the influence of goodness and truth that comes from the Lord and the subsequent spiritual life, which is granted by means of regeneration.

From mercy, the Lord grants us whatever is needed for a life of eternal happiness. *A thousand* stands for a large quantity, so when it is describing divine mercy, it means it is permanent.

8880. *Among those who love me* symbolizes people who are open to loving what is good. This is consistent with the symbolism of *loving Jehovah* (i.e., the Lord) as being an openness to loving what is good. Whoever loves the Lord is not loving him from their own capacity; it comes from the Lord, since everything good flows into us from him. We love him when we stop doing evil, because evil gets in the way and repels that good influence coming from the Lord. Once evil is removed, we can receive the goodness that, thanks to him, is always present and trying to enter us.

8881. *And keep my commandments* symbolizes being open to believing what is true. This is consistent with *commandments* as being a symbol of truths we should believe. *Keeping* that truth symbolizes being receptive to it, since it must flow into us from the Lord in order for us to believe it and so that it can live within us.

Truth can be learned and stored in our memory, but if we do not agree with it and act on it, it does not become living truth. On the other hand, if it is drawn from our memory and embedded in our will by intellectual activity, that is, if we intentionally make it part of our habits and activity, then it becomes living truth—truth that we believe. This is accomplished by the Lord when we stop doing evil, as stated above in §8880.

Verse 7: You Shall Not Utter the Name of Jehovah Your God Unworthily

8882. *You shall not utter the name of Jehovah your God unworthily* symbolizes not profaning and blaspheming what we believe to be good and true. This is consistent with the *name of God* as the symbol of everything we worship in the Lord—everything we believe to be true and good—and with *uttering unworthily* as a symbol of profaning and blaspheming.

Properly understood, *uttering the name of God unworthily* stands for putting the truth to evil purposes, that is, when we know the truth but still engage in evil. Likewise, it is using what is good for false purposes, that is, when we live virtuously but do not believe in virtue. Both are profanation, because we believe according to what we understand but live according to what we want; and for people who believe one thing but do another, what they think and what they want have become separated.

Our will is constantly influencing our intellect, because our intellect is shaped by our will; or in other words, our will is exposed in the light of our intellect. Whenever we think we should do one thing but want to do something else, truth gets connected with evil, or goodness gets connected with falsity. When this happens within someone, heavenly things become combined with infernal things. This combination cannot be dissolved, and thereby the person restored to wholeness, except through a process that completely deprives that person of spiritual life. Accordingly, people like this are sent into the worst of all hells, where they suffer dire things.

[2] This is what is referred to in Matthew by the words,

> People will be forgiven every sin and blasphemy, but blasphemy against the Spirit will not be forgiven. Whoever speaks a word against the Son of Man will be forgiven, but whoever speaks against the Holy Spirit will not be forgiven, either in this age or the age to come. (Matthew 12:31, 32)

And also by these words in Luke,

> When an unclean spirit leaves a person, it wanders through waterless regions looking for a resting place, but not finding any it says, "I will return to my house from which I came." When it comes, it finds it swept and put in order. Then it goes and brings seven other spirits more evil than itself, and they enter and live there; and the last state of that person is worse than the first. (Luke 11:24–26)

[3] These words are a description of how we profane the truth that comes from the Lord. *When an unclean spirit leaves* means acknowledging and believing the truth, and a *home swept* means living contrary to the truth.

His *returning with seven other spirits* refers to the stages of profanation. This is what is meant by *uttering the name of God unworthily*. A person in such a state of mind cannot be made whole and therefore cannot be forgiven. This is what is meant by the words that immediately follow: *Jehovah will not render innocent the person who utters his name unworthily*. This means that it cannot be forgiven.

[4] *Uttering the name of God unworthily* also stands for blasphemy, which happens when something in the Word, or something holy within the body of teachings about faith, is

treated with mockery and dragged down into the dirt and defiled. . . .

[5] *Will not render innocent* means that people who take the name of Jehovah God in vain cannot be forgiven. This is consistent with the words of Jehovah in Moses about such people:

> Whoever has sinned against me I will blot out of my book. But now go, lead the people to the place about which I have spoken to you; see, my angel shall go in front of you. Nevertheless, when the day comes for punishment, I will punish them for their sin. (Exodus 32:32–34)

8883. *Because Jehovah will not render innocent the person who utters his name unworthily* is symbolic of the fact that profanation and blasphemy cannot be forgiven. This is apparent from the explanation in §8882, above.

Verses 8–11: Remember the Sabbath Day, to Consecrate It

8884. *Remember the Sabbath day, to consecrate it. Six days you shall labor and do all your work. And the seventh day is a Sabbath to Jehovah your God; you shall not do any work—you or your son or your daughter, your male servant or your female servant, or your beast, or the foreigner who is in your gates. For in six days Jehovah made the heaven and the earth, the sea, and everything that is in them, and rested on the seventh day. Therefore Jehovah blessed the Sabbath day and consecrated it.*

Remember means to keep it constantly in mind.

At the highest [heavenly] level of meaning, *Sabbath day* stands for the union of the Lord's actual divinity with his deified human manifestation. The inner [spiritual] meaning of it is the connection between his deified human manifestation and the heavens, and so it also means heaven and the marriage between goodness and truth in heaven.

To consecrate it stands for not weakening this union in any way.

Six days you shall labor and do all your work stands for the battle that precedes and prepares us for the marriage between goodness and truth.

And the seventh day is a Sabbath for Jehovah your God stands for goodness being implanted into us and the consequent marriage.

You shall not do any work—you or your son or your daughter, your male servant or your female servant, or your beast, or the foreigner who is in your gates signifies that now there can be heaven and blessedness for us in every aspect of our lives, inwardly as well as outwardly.

For in six days Jehovah made heaven and earth, the sea symbolizes the rebirth and rejuvenation of our inner and outward life.

And everything that is in them symbolizes every aspect of our inner and outward life.

And rested on the seventh day is symbolic of the fact that now we are at peace and are good because we love being good.

Therefore Jehovah blessed the Sabbath day is symbolic of the fact that at this point there is a heavenly marriage from the Lord.

And consecrated it means this marriage can never be weakened.

8885. *Remember* obviously means keeping something constantly in mind, because when we say *remember* about something that should never be forgotten, we mean we should always keep it in mind. Something that is always kept in mind is universally sovereign there. We keep it in mind, even when we are thinking about other things and are engaged in other business.

Our thought incorporates many ideas at the same time, because it is formed by a series of ideas entering our mind.

These ideas come to our direct attention, and we focus on them so we can see them with the enlightenment of our inner sight. Everything else is pushed off to the side, becomes obscured, and is not noticed unless we come across something associated with it. These ideas get pushed further and further away, and they do not stay on the same level but drift downward. These are ideas we reject and oppose—evil and false ideas if we are good people and good and true ideas if we are bad people.

[2] There are certain things that we constantly think about; that is, they are universally sovereign in our mind. These are our deepest thoughts. From the perspective of these thoughts, we view the ideas that we are not constantly thinking about (that is, that are not universally sovereign) as though they are outside of us or beneath us and irrelevant, at least at this point. This enables us to select and adopt those ideas that agree with our deeper thoughts. Once these ideas are adopted and ultimately incorporated, our deepest thoughts—the ones that are universally sovereign—are reinforced. In good people, this involves incorporating new truth; in bad people, it involves either incorporating new falsity or using truth for harmful purposes.

[3] Furthermore, it is important to realize that what is universally sovereign in us has actually been implanted into our will. Our will is the innermost part of us, because it is shaped by our love. Whatever we love, we want, and whatever we love above all else is our deepest desire.

Our intellect, on the other hand, functions to express what we want—what we love—to other people; and by organizing ideas in various ways, it also serves to sway their will into agreement with our own. When this happens, our love or motivation flows from our will into intellectual concepts, and it brings them to life and energizes them with a certain kind of inspiration.

[4] In good people, these intellectual concepts are united with the intentions of their will. But in bad people, it is otherwise; their thinking and their desire are in fact connected on a deep level, because their intellect thinks about the evil they want and connects falsity to that evil. However, this agreement is not evident to people in this world, because we have learned from infancy to say something different from what we are thinking and to act differently from the way we want to act.

Another way of saying this is that we learn to separate our inner being from our outer being and to create within this outer being a second will and a second mind that are different from what is in our inner being. Using this outer being, we feign a goodness that is contrary to our inner being, which wants to do evil at that moment and is secretly contemplating it. In the other life, the nature of our inner will and inner mind is as clear as day, because when we are there our outward appearance is taken away and what is within stripped bare.

8886. At the highest level of meaning, *Sabbath day* stands for the union of the Lord's divinity and his deified human manifestation. The inner meaning of the *Sabbath day* is the connection between his deified human manifestation and the heavens, and so it means heaven and the marriage between goodness and truth in heaven.

Because the Sabbath was a symbol for these unions, it was the holiest representation within the Israelite church. It was the one thing they were always to keep in mind, since it constitutes a heavenly life. . . .

8887. *To consecrate it* symbolizes not weakening this union in any way. This is consistent with what was commanded regarding the Sabbath and also with what follows regarding the Sabbath's holiness:

Six days you shall labor and do all your work. And the seventh day is a Sabbath to Jehovah your God; you shall not do any work—you or your son or your daughter, your male servant or your female servant, or your beast, or the foreigner who is in your gates. For in six days Jehovah made the heaven and the earth, the sea, and everything that is in them, and rested on the seventh day. Therefore Jehovah blessed the Sabbath day and consecrated it.

This passage makes it clear that *consecrating the Sabbath* stands for not violating it in any way, but the inner meaning is that we should not weaken what the Sabbath symbolizes: the union of the Lord's divine essence with his human essence, his union with the heavens, and the subsequent combination of goodness and truth in the heavens. When people undermine these principles, their spiritual life perishes, becoming merely an earthly life and eventually a materialistic one. At that point, they are embracing falsity instead of truth and evil instead of good.

8888. *Six days you shall labor and do all your work* is symbolic of the struggle that comes before and prepares us for the marriage of goodness and truth. This is consistent with the symbolism of *six days* as a period of struggle. It is also consistent with *to labor* and *do all your work* as symbolic of doing everything necessary to live—in this case to live spiritually, or in heaven.

[2] Moreover, *the struggle that precedes and prepares us for the heavenly marriage between goodness and truth* refers to a spiritual struggle or test. Before we enter into a heavenly marriage, that is, before we are reborn, we are in a struggle against evil and falsity within ourselves. These must be removed before we can receive the truth and goodness given to us by the Lord. Evil and falsity are removed by believing what is true, since truth not only enables us to learn what is good but also induces us to do it.

This phase, which we refer to as the phase *preceding and preparing us for heavenly marriage*, is the first step for anyone being reborn. But then, when we are being good and the Lord is leading us by means of that good behavior, we are in a heavenly marriage—in fact, we are in heaven, because heavenly marriage is heaven. The prior phase is what the six days preceding the seventh day symbolizes, and the latter phase is what is symbolized by the seventh day.

[3] The *Sabbath* is the symbol of heavenly marriage, which is heaven. This is why in the heavens, they call the Lord's kingdom a continual Sabbath and therefore a continual rest and peace, and there are no longer six days of labor.

8889. *And the seventh day is a Sabbath to Jehovah your God* is symbolic of when goodness is implanted into us and therefore a marriage occurs. This is consistent with *Sabbath* being the symbol for a heavenly marriage (see §8886 above).

Goodness is implanted by means of truth. It is subsequently organized by that truth, and it is not spiritual goodness within us until it is organized by truth. Once it has been organized, there is a heavenly marriage, which is the combination of goodness and truth. This is actually heaven within us, and it is also why the *seventh day* symbolizes a condition of holiness.

8890. *You shall not do any work—you or your son or your daughter, your male servant or female servant, or your beast, or the foreigner in your gates.* This symbolizes that in this marriage between goodness and truth, there is heaven and blessedness in every aspect of our life—both our inner life and our outward life. This is consistent with not doing any work as a symbol for rest and peace and therefore for heaven. When we are in heaven, we are not worried, restless, or anxious; we are blessed.

This is also consistent with *your sons, your daughters, your male servants, your female servants, your beasts, and the foreigner in your gates* as symbolizing every single aspect of our inner and outward life. *You* refers to each of us as individuals. *Son* means our capacity to understand, and *daughter* means our will; and these are the two aspects of our inner being. *Male servant* means our earthly view of truth, and *female servant* means our earthly view of what is good; and these are the two aspects of our outward life. *Beast*, however, stands for our overall inclination, and the *foreigner in our gates* refers to our overall knowledge. Accordingly, this is talking about each and every aspect of our inner and outward life.

8891. *For in six days Jehovah made the heaven and the earth, and the sea* symbolizes the rebirth and revitalization of aspects of our inner and outward being. This is consistent with *six days* as a symbol of a period of struggle. When it speaks of *Jehovah*, that is, the Lord, it symbolizes the work he does with us before we are reborn (see §8888).

Heaven and earth is symbolic of our involvement with the church, or the Lord's kingdom—heaven referring to our inner life and earth to our outward life. We are reborn; that is, we obtain new life and so in both respects are revitalized. The *sea* is a symbol of the sensory capacity that is characteristic of our physical being.

[2] This verse deals with making the seventh day holy and establishing the Sabbath, described in these words,

> In six days Jehovah made the heaven and the earth, the sea, and everything that is in them, and rested on the seventh day. Therefore Jehovah blessed the Sabbath day and consecrated it.

Anyone who does not think beyond the literal meaning cannot help but believe that the creation described in the first and second chapters of Genesis is the creation of the universe and that the six days was a period of time within which were created heaven, the earth, the sea, everything within them, and ultimately humans in the likeness of God.

But how can anyone reflecting on the details in these chapters fail to see that it does not mean the creation of the universe? There are things here that common sense can tell us are not so. For example, how can there be six days before there is a sun and a moon? How can there be light and darkness, or how can plants and trees grow, when it is the illumination of the sun and the moon that produces light, creating a contrast between light and shadow and enabling us to mark out days?

[3] The next verses have similar statements that cannot really be accepted as fact by someone thinking on a deeper level. For example, that woman was constructed from a man's rib; that two trees were planted in paradise, and it was forbidden to eat the fruit of one of them; that the serpent, the wisest of all mortal beings, spoke to the man's wife from one of the trees; and that both the man and the woman were deceived by the speech that came from the mouth of the serpent, because of which the whole human race—millions and millions of people—are condemned to hell. On first consideration, these and similar things can only seem absurd to anyone harboring any hesitation about the Word's holiness, and it can ultimately influence them to deny the Word's divinity.

On the contrary, we should realize that everything in the letter of the Word is divine, down to the least mark. Each contains within itself mysteries that are as clear as day to the angels reading them in heaven. This is because the angels do not see the Word's meaning in the letter; they see it in what is within the letter, the spiritual and heavenly concepts that contain divine principles.

When angels read the first chapter of Genesis, they immediately infer no other creation than the re-creation of a human being, which we call being regenerated. This is what is being described there. By *paradise*, they infer that the wisdom of a person who has been created anew is what is being described. By the *twin trees in its midst*, they infer that the mental faculties of a person who is regenerated are what is being described: the will to do good (the Tree of Life) and the ability to understand truth (the Tree of Knowledge). It was forbidden to eat from this second tree, because a person who is regenerated—or created anew—should no longer be led by an understanding of truth but by the desire to do good. If we do otherwise, our new life perishes.

Consequently, the man—Adam—and his wife—Eve—represent a new church, and *eating of the tree of knowledge* means that new church's lapse away from goodness and toward truth. In this way, they fell away from loving the Lord and loving other people and fell into a faith that lacked that love. This is the result of making rationalizations from our own intelligence. Such rationalizing is the *serpent*.

[4] These examples demonstrate that the story of creation, of the first man, and of the garden of Eden are made-up stories containing within them heavenly and divine concepts. This follows the custom of coming up with stories and incorporating within them hidden meanings—a custom that was practiced in the ancient churches and that spread to many outside the church, as we can discern from reading the authors of those ancient cultures.

In the ancient churches, they understood what things in this world symbolize in heaven. They were not much concerned with representing actual events but rather with their heavenly meaning. This occupied their minds, because they were thinking on a deeper level than people do today. They were communicating with angels, and they enjoyed making connections between earthly and heavenly things. Truly, they were being led by the Lord toward concepts that needed to be kept sacred in those churches. This resulted in stories that were beautifully rendered, with a perfect correspondence between earthly and heavenly things.

[5] We can deduce from this what *the heaven and the earth* means in the first verse of chapter 1 of Genesis: it means the inner church and the outward church. This symbolism of *the heaven and the earth* is consistent with passages in the Prophets, where it talks about *a new heaven and a new earth*.

This makes it clear that *in six days Jehovah made the heaven and the earth, and the sea* symbolizes the rebirth and revitalization of aspects of our inner and outward being.

8892. *And everything that is in them* means that everything in our inner and outward being is revitalized. This should be obvious without explanation.

8893. *And rested on the seventh day* symbolizes the point at which we are at peace and are good people by virtue of the goodness of love. This is consistent with *to rest* as a symbol for peace and *seventh day* as a symbol for achieving a state of celestial love (and also a symbol for the holiness that comes from that state).

Before we are reborn, or created anew, we are in a state of anxiety and agitation. Our earthly habits are battling against our spiritual habits and want to dominate them. This is why the Lord is laboring at this stage; he is fighting on our behalf against the hells that are attacking us.

But as soon as the goodness of love is implanted into us, the battle stops and we find rest. We are led into heaven and guided by the Lord according to heaven's laws of order, and as a result we find peace. This is the symbolism of *Jehovah rested on the seventh day*.

8894. *Therefore Jehovah blessed the Sabbath day* is symbolic of the heavenly marriage created at that point by the Lord. This is consistent with *to bless* as a symbol for being brought into heavenly order and being endowed with the goodness of love. It is also consistent with *the Sabbath day* as a symbol of achieving a state of heavenly love and therefore a heavenly marriage. Heavenly marriage is the combining of goodness and truth, and this creates heaven within us.

8895. *And consecrated it* symbolizes that it cannot be violated in any way. When talking about the heavenly marriage within a person who has been regenerated, it means that this heavenly marriage cannot be violated (see §8887). The Lord's holiness within us cannot be violated, as long as we accept the Lord's holiness, that is, as long as we are in the goodness of love, or in other words, as long as we are in heaven.

Verse 12: Honor Your Father and Your Mother

8896. *Honor your father and your mother, in order that your days may lengthen on the land that Jehovah your God is giving you.*

This is symbolic of loving what is good and true. At the highest level of meaning, that means loving the Lord and his kingdom.

In order that your days may lengthen on the land is a symbol for living in heaven.

That Jehovah your God is giving you symbolizes where the deity is and its resulting influence.

8897. *Honor your father and your mother* is symbolic of loving what is good and true; and at its highest level of meaning, this means loving the Lord and his kingdom. This is consistent with *to honor* as a symbol for loving.

The spiritual meaning of *honor* is love, because in heaven they love one another and in so doing they honor one another. Within honor there is love, and in heaven they refuse to be honored unless there is love in it; in fact, they denounce it, because it is not alive with goodwill.

This interpretation is also consistent with *father* as a symbol for goodness. At its highest level of meaning, this refers to the Lord in regard to his divine goodness. The reason why at its highest level of meaning the Lord is father is that he gives us new life; and through this new life, he makes us *his sons and heirs to his kingdom.*

It is also consistent with *mother* as a symbol for truth. At its highest level of meaning, this refers to the Lord in regard to divine truth; and therefore, it refers to his kingdom, since the divine truth that comes from the Lord constitutes heaven. The reason the Lord's divine truth constitutes heaven is that in the other life, he is the sun in regard to divine goodness and the light in regard to divine truth. This divine light coming from the Lord as their sun is what enlightens the minds of angels and fills them with intelligence and wisdom, making them angels of light. Divine goodness is within divine truth, as heat from the sun is within the light of springtime and summertime in this world.

8898. *In order that your days may lengthen on the land* is symbolic of our life in heaven. This is consistent with *to lengthen* as a symbol referring to becoming a better person (more on that below); with *your days* as a symbol of the state of mind we are in; and also with *land*, which refers in this passage to the land of Canaan (because it is being said to the children of Israel *that Jehovah your God is giving you [this land]*), as a symbol of the Lord's kingdom.

To lengthen refers to becoming a better person. A *lengthening of our days* means living a long time; but in heaven there is no time and space, so this is talking about the state of mind of people in heaven. *In order that your days may lengthen* means becoming a better person, because *lengthen* describes the intensification of their positive state of mind.

8899. *That Jehovah your God is giving you* symbolizes where the deity is and its resulting influence. This is consistent with what we said about heaven (symbolized here by *land*) in the preceding section. Jehovah God is the deity that is there;

and *give* means the divine influence, because heaven consists of each person—individually and as a group—receiving the deity's influence.

It might seem strange that this commandment about honoring one's parents is a symbol of these kinds of ideas, because they are so different from the literal meaning. It is important to realize, however, that the principles of the Ten Commandments are intended as rules both for those in this world and those in heaven. The literal, or surface, meaning is intended for those who live in this world; and the spiritual, or inner, meaning is intended for those in heaven. Of course, both meanings—the inner and the surface—are intended for those who, while living in this world, are also in heaven, that is, who lead good lives based on what they have been taught to be true.

That the principles of the Ten Commandments are intended for people in heaven is obvious from the inner meaning of everything said in the Word. The fact that Jehovah God himself (the Lord) said these things means that they are intended not only for us in this world but also for the angels and indeed all of heaven. The divine truth that comes from the Lord passes through heaven and spreads throughout it until it reaches us [in the world]. And so this is true for the principles of the Ten Commandments, which the Lord himself spoke from Mount Sinai.

[2] Since the Ten Commandments are intended not only for people in this world but also for people in heaven, they cannot mean the same thing to both groups. Take, for example, this commandment that we should *honor our father and mother in order that our days may lengthen on the land that Jehovah God is giving us.* In heaven, parents and children do not live together as they do on earth; and therefore, their father is the Lord and their mother is his kingdom. Because

they live to eternity, people in heaven do not say that their days are lengthened. And they do not understand the concept of *land*, such as the land of Canaan in this commandment. For them, *land* means the heavenly Canaan, that is, heaven.

Since *father and mother* means the Lord and his kingdom, this commandment is the fourth in the series and surpasses in holiness the ones that come after it. The commandment about worshipping Jehovah (that is, the Lord) is first and second, because it is the holiest. Next comes the commandment about the Sabbath, because at the highest level of meaning it is a symbol of the union within the Lord of his divinity and his deified human manifestation.

The commandment about honoring parents comes next, because it is a symbol of loving the Lord and therefore a symbol of his giving us a love of what is good and true. Because these ideas are symbolized by this commandment, having contempt for parents is considered disgraceful, which is symbolized by *pouring out blood* (Ezekiel 22:6–7) and by *disobedient and defiant sons being stoned* (Deuteronomy 21:18–22).

8900. Just above (§8897), we showed how *father* means the Lord and *mother* means his kingdom. If, for some reason, it is hard to accept the Lord's kingdom—or heaven—as the inner meaning of *mother*, allow me to add this. In the Word, *mother* means the church, which is also called *the bride and wife of the Lord*. The Lord's kingdom is the same thing as the church—the sole difference being that the Lord's kingdom on earth is called the church—and so it is also symbolized by *mother*. The sons born of that mother are truths and are called *sons of the realm* in Matthew 13:38. For everyone in heaven, their country is the Lord's kingdom. Our country is our mother in an earthly sense in the same way that the church is our mother in a spiritual sense.

Verse 13: You Shall Not Kill

8901. *You shall not kill* symbolizes not depriving another person of their spiritual life, not stifling their faith or their goodwill, and also not hating our neighbor.

8902. *To kill* means to deprive someone of their spiritual life. This is the inner meaning of *to kill*, because the inner meaning deals with spiritual life—or life in heaven. Since our spiritual life—or our life in heaven—is living in faith and goodwill, *not to kill* also symbolizes not stifling anyone's faith or goodwill.

Another reason the inner meaning of *do not kill* is to not hate our neighbor is that when we do so we are perpetually wanting to kill that person; and we would physically do it, if we did not fear punishment, losing our own life, losing our reputation, and the like. Hatred comes from evil, the opposite of goodwill, and wants nothing but the death of those we hate. In this world, that means the death of their body; in the other life, it means the death of their soul. This is what the words of the Lord in Matthew mean:

> You have heard that it was said to those of ancient times, "You shall not kill. Whoever kills will be liable to judgment." But I say to you that if you are angry with a brother or sister, you will be liable to judgment; and if you insult a brother or sister, you will be liable to the council; and if you say, "You fool," you will be liable to the hell of fire. (Matthew 5:21–22)

Being *angry with a brother or sister* means hating your neighbor. Insulting someone and calling them *a fool* describe increased levels of anger.

[2] In the Word, nearly every passage in which *killing* is mentioned confirms the inner meaning of *killing* as depriving someone of spiritual life and stifling their faith and goodwill.

For example, in Isaiah:

> See, the day of the Lord comes, cruel, with wrath and fierce anger, to make the earth a desolation, and to destroy its sinners from it. For the stars of the heavens and their constellations will not give their light; the sun will be dark at its rising, and the moon will not shed its light. I will punish the world for its evil, and the wicked for their iniquity; I will put an end to the pride of the arrogant, and lay low the insolence of tyrants. I will make humans more rare than fine gold, and the sons of humankind than the gold of Ophir. . . . Whoever is found will be thrust through, and whoever is caught will fall by the sword. Their infants will be dashed to pieces before their eyes; their houses will be plundered, and their wives ravished. . . . Their bows will slaughter the young men; they will have no mercy on the fruit of the womb; their eyes will not pity the sons. (Isaiah 13:9–18)

This is talking about the last stage of the church, when there is no longer faith and goodwill. This stage is *the day of the Lord, cruel, with wrath and fierce anger.* Anyone can see that this means something other than what the mere words indicate, but the meaning can only be discerned from the symbolism of the words. *To make the earth a desolation, and to destroy its sinners from it* is symbolic of the church member who in the last stage of the church lacks faith and goodwill.

[3] *Stars* and *constellations* are our awareness of what is true and good. When people are no longer enlightened by the light of heaven, which flows into us through our belief in goodwill, it is said that they *do not give their light.*

The *sun* means loving the Lord, and the *moon* means believing in him. Therefore, *the sun will be dark at its rising* symbolizes when it is no longer possible for someone to love the Lord, and *the moon will not shed its light* symbolizes when it is no longer possible to be kind and have faith in the Lord. In other words, the person is no longer able to be regenerated.

[4] To *make humans more rare than fine gold, and the sons of humankind than the gold of Ophir* is symbolic of the fact that we can no longer see what is good or what is true. *Humans* are a symbol for what is good in the church. The *sons of humankind* are a symbol of truth that comes from being good, and at the highest level of meaning it means divine truth coming from the Lord.

Whoever is found will be thrust through is symbolic of the fact that everyone perishes from the evil that results from falsity, and *whoever is caught will fall by the sword* is symbolic of perishing as a result of falsity.

[5] Since *infants* means innocence, infants being *dashed to pieces* is symbolic of that innocence being completely extinguished. *Their wives ravished* is symbolic of the fact that good impulses inspired by truth will be perverted by evil impulses inspired by falsity.

Their bows will slaughter the young men is symbolic of the truth that comes from being good perishing as a result of false teaching that comes from evil. A *bow* is truthful teaching, but in a negative sense it is false teaching; *young men* is truth that we have confirmed. Because *sons* means the truth, *their eyes will not pity the sons* is symbolic of someone who understands the truth but nevertheless stifles it. The *eye* is the ability to understand the truth.

This clarifies the words of the prophet: when the church comes to an end, all truthfulness and good intention will perish. It also demonstrates that to be *thrust through* and *dashed to pieces*, in other words to be killed, means the loss of faith and goodwill. . . .

[17] From these symbols, and others, we can confirm that there are mysteries contained within every detail of the Word;

and there are a great many of them. Nor will we even recognize them as mysteries, if we believe that the literal meaning is all there is to the Word and that there is nothing more holy and heavenly lying hidden within. Yet the truth is that there is a literal meaning for people in this world—that is, earthly people—but an inner meaning for people in heaven—that is, spiritual people.

And so it is obvious what this commandment against killing involves: not only should we not kill someone physically, but we should not kill in respect to the soul. Not only should people not be deprived of life in this world, but even more importantly, they should not be deprived of a life in heaven.

If the commandment against killing did not include this latter point, it would not have been so miraculously decreed aloud by Jehovah himself (that is, the Lord) from Mount Sinai. Even without the aid of revelation, all peoples and nations know and ordain by law that people should not kill, just as they should not commit adultery, should not steal, and should not give false testimony. Neither should we think that the Israelite nation was so stupid that it alone did not know this, when every other nation in the entire world knew it. The revealed Word conceals an even deeper and more universal truth, because it is from a divine source. These are heavenly matters that are relevant not just to the life of the body but also to the life of the soul—eternal life. In this respect, the Word differs from, surpasses, and transcends any other written work.

Verse 13: You Shall Not Commit Adultery

8903. *You shall not commit adultery* means that we should not pervert the teachings about faith and goodwill, using the Word to confirm what is evil and false and ultimately standing the laws of order on their head.

8904. This meaning is consistent with the symbolism of *to seduce, to commit adultery,* and *to fornicate.* Their spiritual, or inner, meaning is to pervert what is good and falsify what is true when teaching about faith and goodwill. Since *committing adultery* is a symbol for doing this, it also symbolizes using the Word to confirm what is evil and false. The Word is what actually teaches us about faith and goodwill, and so perverting what is true and good in the Word means that we are using it for false and evil purposes.

Hardly anyone today knows that the terms *to seduce* or *to commit adultery* have this spiritual meaning. This is because few people in the church today know that there is a spiritual realm and how it differs from this earthly realm. Barely anyone knows that there is a correspondence between the two realms and that the one is mirrored in the other; that is, the spiritual realm is represented within the earthly realm. As a result, they do not know that the spiritual realm is like the soul and the earthly realm is like its body. As the spiritual realm flows into the earthly realm, the two realms connect and make one. This is just like what happens between the inner, or spiritual, being and the outward, or earthly, being of a person who is regenerated.

[2] Since such concepts are unknown at the present day, it is impossible for people to know what is meant by *committing adultery,* beyond an illicit physical coupling. But because these ideas are unknown, permit me to state why *committing adultery* in its spiritual meaning symbolizes perverting the teaching about faith and goodwill and so also polluting what is good and falsifying what is true.

The answer, which these days is a secret one, is that marriage love flows down from the marriage between what is good and what is true, which is called *heavenly marriage.* The love that flows in from the Lord and that in heaven is a love between what is good and what is true, on earth turns into marriage love; and it does so by correspondence. This is why the inner meaning of *whoredom* is to falsify the truth, and the inner meaning of *adultery* is to pervert goodness. It is also why people who do not believe in what is good and true cannot enjoy a genuine love in their marriage. Ultimately, it is why people for whom engaging in adultery is the delight of their life are no longer open to faith.

I have heard it said by angels that as soon as someone commits adultery on earth and enjoys it, heaven is closed to that person. In other words, the individual refuses from that point on to accept any faith and goodwill from heaven.

At the present day, in the realms where the church exists, most people think that adultery is inconsequential. This is because the church is in its end stage. There is no faith, because there is no goodwill—the one corresponding to the other. When there is no faith, falsity replaces truth and evil replaces goodness; and we are led to believe that adultery should no longer be considered disgraceful. This is the kind of thinking that hell induces when heaven has been closed off within us.

[3] The inner, or spiritual, meaning of *to seduce* and *to commit adultery* is to pervert the belief in what is true and good and then to confirm what is false and evil by taking things from the Word out of context. We can verify this wherever *seducing, committing adultery*, or *fornicating* is mentioned in the Word—as is quite obvious from the following passages. For example, in Ezekiel,

> Son of man, make known to Jerusalem her abominations . . .
> You trusted in your beauty, and played the whore because of
> your fame, and lavished your whorings on any passer-by. You
> took some of your garments, and made for yourself colorful

shrines, and on them played the whore; nothing like this has ever been or ever shall be. You also took your beautiful vessels of my gold and my silver that I had given you, and made for yourself male images, and with them played the whore . . . You took your sons and your daughters, whom you had borne to me, and these you sacrificed to them to be devoured. As if your whorings were not enough! . . . You played the whore with the Egyptians, your lustful neighbors, multiplying your whoring, to provoke me to anger. . . . You played the whore with the Assyrians, because you were insatiable; you played the whore with them, and still you were not satisfied. You multiplied your whoring with Chaldea, the land of merchants; and even with this you were not satisfied. . . . Adulterous wife, who receives strangers instead of her husband! Gifts are given to all whores; but you gave your gifts to all your lovers, bribing them to come to you from all around for your whorings. . . . Therefore, O whore, hear the word of Jehovah . . . I will judge you as women who commit adultery and shed blood are judged. (Ezekiel 16:2, 15–17, 20, 26, 28–29, 32–33, 35, 38)

[4] Who cannot see that *whoredom* in this passage is a symbol for falsifying what is true and polluting what is good? Who can understand a word of this without knowing that *whoredom* symbolizes such things? Or without knowing what is symbolized by *the Egyptians, the Assyrians*, or *Chaldea*, all with whom Jerusalem is said to fornicate? It is obvious that Jerusalem did not actually fornicate with these people, and so the inner meaning needs to be explained.

Jerusalem means a church that has been perverted. In this passage, *garments* are the truth that the church is perverting, and the false concepts that it subsequently embraces are the *colorful shrines*. *The Egyptians* are learned facts; *the Assyrians* are reasoned ideas; and *Chaldea* means profaning the truth.

Beautiful vessels of my gold and my silver means recognizing what is good and true. *Male images* symbolizes appearances and likenesses of truth. *Your sons and your daughters, whom you had borne to me* refers to the good and true things they have perverted, and *the Egyptians* refers to the facts they used in perverting the truth. *Assyrians* refers to the reasoning by which, using those facts, their belief in the truth was perverted and their belief in what is good was polluted. *Multiplied your whoring with Chaldea* means this goes on until the truth is profaned. It becomes obvious, then, why Chaldea is called *an adulterous woman* and *a whore.*

[5] Similar things are said about Babylon in the book of Revelation,

> Then one of the seven angels who had the seven vessels came and said to me, "Come, I will show you the judgment of the great whore who is seated on many waters, with whom the kings of the earth have committed fornication, and with the wine of whose fornication the inhabitants of the earth have become drunk." (Revelation 17:1–2; see also 17:5, 14:8, 18:3)

Babylon refers to people who pervert what is true and good in the church in order to gain control or to enrich themselves. They do this until profanation occurs, as we can conclude from the symbolism of *Babel.* . . .

[12] These passages clearly show the symbolism of *committing adultery.* On the surface, it means to commit adultery, but its inner representative meaning is to employ the church's teachings to worship idols and other gods, which is both outward and inward idolatry. In its inner spiritual meaning, it stands for adulterating what is good and perverting what is true.

This explains why adultery is intrinsically so awful, and it is called an abomination. All adultery corresponds to a marriage between what is false and what is evil, which is infernal marriage. On the other hand, this is why real marriage is so holy: it corresponds to the marriage between what is good and what is true, which is celestial marriage. In fact, genuine marriage love descends from this marriage between what is good and what is true, and so it comes from heaven—or from the Lord through heaven. Adulterous love comes from the marriage between what is false and what is evil, and so it comes from hell—or from the devil.

Verse 13: You Shall Not Steal

8905. *You shall not steal* symbolizes not taking away anyone's spiritual values, or attributing to oneself what belongs to the Lord.

8906. The reason *you shall not steal* has this symbolism is due to *stealing* being a symbol for taking away someone's spiritual values. The spiritual meaning of riches and wealth is an awareness of what is good and what is true. These values are basically anything that has to do with our faith and our goodwill toward others, and therefore they relate to our spiritual life. Taking these away from someone is the spiritual meaning of *stealing*.

All of our spiritual values—everything relating to our faith and our goodwill toward others—come solely from the Lord. Absolutely none of them come from ourselves. Accordingly, *stealing* is also a symbol for attributing to ourselves what belongs to the Lord. Such people are called *thieves* and *robbers* in John,

> Very truly, I tell you, anyone who does not enter the sheepfold by the gate but climbs in by another way is a thief and a bandit. The one who enters by the gate is the shepherd of the sheep. . . . I am the gate . . . Whoever enters by me will be saved, and will come in and go out and find pasture. The thief comes only to steal and kill and destroy. I came that they may have life, and have it abundantly. (John 10:1–10)

To *enter the sheepfold by the gate* means entering by means of the Lord, since he is the *gate*, as he himself says. The *sheep* are people who have goodwill and therefore also have faith. They *enter by the Lord* when they recognize that all aspects of faith and goodwill toward others come entirely from him, since it is from him that these things influence us.

Yet when we attribute these values to some other source— especially if we attribute them to ourselves—that is *stealing*, and likewise *killing* them and *destroying* them. People who attribute these values to themselves also take credit for the good works they do and claim they are justified by them.

So this is the spiritual meaning of *stealing*; and, for the angels in heaven, this is what comes to mind when we on earth read about *stealing* in the Word. For the angels, the Word has only a spiritual meaning.

[2] This concept is symbolized in Hosea,

> When I saved Israel, then the corruption of Ephraim was revealed, and the wicked deeds of Samaria; because they acted falsely, the thief broke in and the band rushed out the doors. . . . Now their deeds surround them openly before my face. By their wickedness they make the king glad, and by their falsehoods the chiefs. (Hosea 7:1–3)

And also in Joel,

> The day of Jehovah is coming . . . before him the fire consumes and after him the flame burns. Before him the land is like the garden of Eden, but after him a desert wasteland . . . His appearance is like the appearance of horses, and as horses they run, as the thunder of chariots upon the mountain tops. . . . They run about in the city, they run upon the wall, they climb up into houses and enter through the windows like a thief. The land quaked before him, the heavens trembled, the sun and the moon were darkened, and the stars withdrew their shining. (Joel 2:1–10)

It is talking here about the desolation of the church, when false ideas abound and obliterate the truth. These false ideas are *thieves who climb up into the houses and enter by the windows.*

Who does not wonder why it says the day of Jehovah *will be like the appearance of horses* and that *at that time as horses run, they will run through the city, they will run upon the wall, they will climb up into the houses, they will enter through the windows, the land will quake, the heavens will tremble, the sun and the moon will be darkened,* and *the stars will withdraw their shining?* People who know nothing about the inner meaning and who question the Word's holiness may say that these are just ordinary words without any divine meaning concealed within them, or maybe they will say that they are meaningless phrases.

On the other hand, those who believe that the Word is most holy because it is divine and who also know that it has an inner meaning that teaches us about the church, about heaven, and about the Lord himself will appreciate that each word is important in its own right. Accordingly, we should say a few things about what the words and phrases in this passage stand for.

[3] The *day of Jehovah* means the last stage, or end time, of the church. There is no longer truth; it has been replaced by falsity.

The *fire that consumes before him* is the desire for evil. The *flame that burns after him* is the accompanying desire for falsity.

The *appearance of horses* means intellectual reasoning from false principles as though they were the truth. Those who *run like horses* are people who reason in this way.

The *chariot* means teaching what is false. The *city* is the actual teaching, and the *wall upon which they run* is the underlying falsity.

The *homes that they climb up into* is our voluntary faculty.

The *windows through which they enter* means intellectual concepts.

The *thief* is falsity that takes away the truth.

The *land that will quake before him* means the church, as does the *heavens that will tremble*.

The *sun* means our love of the Lord; the *moon* means our faith in the Lord; and they are said to be *darkened* when we no longer heed them.

The *stars* means our awareness of what is good and true; and when we no longer have the light of faith and love (that is, light from heaven), the stars *withdraw their shining*.

From these symbols, we can derive the overall context of the passage and figure out why that day—the last stage of the church—is called the *thief who will climb up into the houses and enter through the windows:* in the last stage of the church, falsehood will take total possession of both our voluntary and intellectual faculties and therefore will take away everything good and true. The same concept is symbolized by *thief* in Obadiah,

> The Lord Jehovah said to Edom . . . If thieves come to you, if plunderers by night, how have you been destroyed? Would they not steal only what they wanted? (Obadiah 1:1, 5)

Similar things are said about the *thief*, or *thieving*, in Zechariah 5:1–4, Psalms 50:18–20, and Matthew 6:19–20.

[4] All the regulations the Lord issued to the children of Israel were based on the laws of order that apply in heaven. In other words, these regulations draw their substance from and are sustained by the spiritual world. This is the case for what is said about thieves, as for that,

> Whoever has stolen a cow and sells it, let him pay five times the price, but if a sheep, four times. (Exodus 22:1)

Also,

> If a thief is struck down while breaking in, there shall be no blood penalty. However, if the sun is risen, blood is required. . . . The thief must pay or be sold. . . . If what he has stolen is found in his hand, he must pay double. (Exodus 22:2, 7)

> Whoever kidnaps a person to sell him, but that person is still in his hand, shall be put to death. (Exodus 21:16)

> If a man is found who has kidnapped a fellow soul of the children of Israel, to make money by selling him, the thief must be killed to remove the evil from your midst. (Deuteronomy 24:7)

The inner meaning of a *man of the children of Israel* is an individual who believes in what is true and good. In an abstract sense, it is faith in what is true and good; so *stealing a man of the children of Israel* means the loss of that faith, and *selling him* means becoming foreign to it and being subjected to slavery. Since our faith in what is true and good comes from the Lord, [when we have faith] we are in a state of freedom and serve no one but the Lord alone. Yet when we are alienated from this belief, we come into a state of servitude, becoming a slave to whatever evil arises from self-love or worldly ambition—ultimately some bodily craving.

This enables us to derive the correspondence of this law: at this stage, what is true and good in the church goes from a state of freedom to a state of slavery, and so it goes from being a living thing to being dead. The penalty, which is the result, is death.

Verse 13: You Shall Not Testify as a Lying Witness against Your Neighbor

8907. *You shall not testify as a lying witness against your neighbor* symbolizes that something good should not be called bad or that something true should not be called false; and the other way around, something evil should not be called good or something false should not be called true.

8908. This symbolism is consistent with *testifying as a lying witness* being a symbol of confirming what is false. *Testimony* is a confirmation, and the following arguments will make it clear that *lying testimony* means putting our faith in what is false. To *testify against your neighbor* is to confirm something false in speaking to another person, because *neighbor* is a symbol for any other person. More specifically, *neighbor* means a person who is doing good; and in an abstract sense, it means the actual good that that person does. Consequently, the inner meaning of *you shall not testify as a lying witness against your neighbor* is to not speak falsely, that is, to not claim that something good is bad or that something true is false, and vice versa.

[2] I should briefly explain how this works: people governed by their self-love or worldly ambition, whose goal in life is to have control and be esteemed or to have a lavish lifestyle and be wealthy, do not care if they give false testimony by persuading people to believe that something unjust is just. Their will is totally subject to their passions and their cravings, and it is completely preoccupied and obsessed with them. As a result, the other half of their mind—their intellect—which is able to discern what is just and what is unjust, nevertheless chooses not to do so. Their will overrules their intellect by infiltrating it, persuading it, and ultimately blinding it. People like this have no conscience. They do not know that it is a matter of conscience to call just what is just—for no other reason than that it is so, that is, from love of justice.

People who are like this in the world are also just like this in the other life. The difference is that in the other life, they do not claim that something just is unjust. Instead, since justice in our civil realm corresponds to what is good and true in the spiritual realm, they claim that it is bad to believe in what is good and wrong to believe in what is true. They do this without conscience and without shame, because they are so absorbed and comfortable in material living.

[3] *Lying* is mentioned many times in the Word; and wherever it occurs, its inner meaning is to believe in falsity and evil. *Testimony of a lying witness*, also referred to as the *testimony of violence*, stands for confirming what is false—whether it is in front of a judge, in front of any other person, or to ourselves when we persuade ourselves within our own thoughts (Exodus 23:1–7; Leviticus 19:11–12; Deuteronomy 19:16–20).

The following passages demonstrate that the inner meaning of *lying* is to believe what is evil and false:

> You are of your father the devil, and you wish to do your father's desires. He was a murderer from the beginning, and has not stood in the truth, because the truth was not in him. When he speaks a lie, he speaks according to his own nature, because he is a liar and the father of lies. (John 8:44)

In this passage, *lie* stands for believing what is false. It is talking about the Jews not wanting to accept the Lord. The spiritual meaning of *devil* here is falsehood; and *the father of lies* means evil, since falsehood comes from evil as a son comes from the father. Falsity that is *of the devil* is the belief in what is false, and the evil it comes from is the evil of self-love and worldly ambition.

[4] In Isaiah,

> How proud Moab has become, his glory, his pride, and his insolence. His lies are not strong. (Isaiah 16:6)

Lies stand for false ideas that we believe, since *Moab* stands for people who love themselves and therefore who falsify the truth.

Also in Isaiah,

> We have made a covenant with death, and made a common vision with hell. We have placed our trust in lies, and have taken refuge in falsity. (Isaiah 28:15)

. . . In these and so many other passages, *lying* means putting our faith in falsity and evil.

Verse 14: You Shall Not Covet Your Neighbor's House; You Shall Not Covet Your Neighbor's Wife, or His Male Servant or His Female Servant, or His Ox or His Donkey

8909. The symbolism of *you shall not covet your neighbor's house; you shall not covet your neighbor's wife, or his male servant or his female servant, or his ox or his donkey, or anything that is your neighbor's* is to beware of our self-love and worldly ambition so that the evil impulses covered in the preceding commandments do not become intentional in us and come out in our actions.

8910. This symbolism is consistent with *coveting* meaning a wish that is motivated by evil love. It has this meaning because coveting or craving comes entirely from some kind of love. We do not crave anything that we do not love. Craving is an extension of love—in this case, self-love or worldly ambition. Love can be compared to the life force behind our breathing: what an evil love breathes out is what we call coveting or craving, whereas what a good love breathes out is what we call desire. Since we want whatever we love, love itself affects the half of the mind that we call the will. Craving, on the other hand, affects both halves—the will and the intellect; though properly speaking, it is our will functioning within our intellect.

This should clarify why the words *you shall not covet what belongs to your neighbor* mean to make sure evil does not become intentional. We are responsible for the evil that comes from our will, since, in fact, our will is who we really are.

[2] The world believes that we are what we think, when in fact there are two faculties that make up our life: our intellect and our will. Thinking is in the domain of our intellect, but what we tend to love belongs to our will. Thinking that is separated from what we tend to love does not animate us at all; thinking inspired by love—when our intellect is inspired by our will—does.

Anyone who thinks about it can confirm that these are two distinct faculties. We are able to recognize and understand when something we want is evil or when something we either want or do not want is good. Obviously, then, our will is actually who we are, but our thinking is not, except to the extent that our thoughts come from our will. This is why what enters our thought but does not pass into our will does not make us unclean, yet what enters our will from our thinking does. This renders us unclean, because we are now responsible for it since it becomes our own. As mentioned previously, our will is who we actually are. What belongs to our will is said to enter our heart and therefore can go out from the heart; however, what belongs to our thoughts is said to enter into the mouth but to pass through the stomach and into the sewer, according to the Lord's words in Matthew,

> It is not what goes into the mouth that defiles a person, but it is what comes out of the mouth that defiles. . . . Do you not see that whatever goes into the mouth enters the stomach, and goes out into the sewer? But what comes out of the mouth proceeds from the heart, and this is what defiles. For out of the heart come evil intentions, murder, adultery, fornication, theft, false witness, slander. (Matthew 15:11, 17–19)

[3] From these and all other passages, we can characterize how the Lord spoke: he is talking about inner, or spiritual, ideas; but they are expressed through superficial, or earthly, concepts. This is done by correspondences. For example, *mouth* corresponds to our thought, as does everything that has to do with the mouth: the lips, the tongue, the throat. *Heart* corresponds to what we tend to love and therefore to our will.

Accordingly, to *go into the mouth* means it enters our thoughts, and to *come from the heart* means it comes from our will. To *enter the stomach and go out into the sewer* means it is cast into hell, because the stomach corresponds to the pathway to hell and the sewer or toilet to hell. (In the Word, hell is even referred to as a latrine.) The symbolism is obvious: *everything that goes into the mouth enters the stomach, and goes out into the sewer* means that evil and falsity are introduced into us from hell, and they are relegated back to that place.

Because they are relegated to hell, this evil and falsity cannot render us unclean. We cannot help thinking about it, but we can resist doing it. Yet the moment we voluntarily accept the evil we are thinking about, it is not leaving us but is entering us. This is referred to as *entering into the heart*. What comes from the heart renders us unclean, because what we intend comes out in our speech and actions—at least to the extent that it is not held in check by external bonds such as fear of the law, of losing our reputation, of losing respect, of losing money, or of losing our life.

This should make it clear that *you shall not covet* means watching out so that evil does not become voluntary and then come out in our actions.

[4] The Lord's words in Matthew also demonstrate that *coveting* comes from the will and therefore from the heart,

You have heard that it was said by men of ancient times, "You shall not commit adultery," but I say to you that everyone who looks at a woman with lust has already committed adultery with her in his heart. (Matthew 5:27, 29)

In this passage, *lusting [after]*, or coveting, something means willing it and then—so long as one is not held back by the external bonds of fear—acting on that desire. This is why it says *everyone who looks at a woman with lust has already committed adultery with her in his heart.*

[5] In Matthew, the Lord's words about the *right eye that causes you to sin* also refer to craving evil, and the *right hand that causes you to sin* means craving falsity,

If your right eye causes you to sin, tear it out and throw it away; it is better for you to lose one of your members than for your whole body to be thrown into Gehenna. And if your right hand causes you to sin, cut it off and throw it away; it is better for you to lose one of your members than for your whole body to go to Gehenna. (Matthew 5:29, 30)

This passage again demonstrates the nature of the Lord's speech and that he is speaking from a divine source, as is the case in every such passage in the Word. Inner [spiritual] and heavenly ideas are being expressed by superficial, or earthly, concepts by means of correspondence. In this case, an inclination toward evil, a craving for it, is represented by the *right eye that causes you to sin*. An inclination toward falsity, a lust for it, is represented by the *right hand that causes you to sin*. *Eye* corresponds to our faith, and the *left eye* means to believe in what is true. The *right eye* means to believe in what is good; but the negative meaning is to believe in what is evil, so the *right eye that causes you to sin* corresponds to craving what is evil.

The *hand*, though, corresponds to the power of truth. The *right hand* corresponds to the power of truth from a good motivation, but the negative meaning is the power of falsity from a bad motivation. The *right hand that causes you to sin*, therefore, corresponds to lusting after the power of falsity from a bad motivation. *Gehenna* is the hell of cravings.

Anyone can see that the *right eye* in this passage does not mean our right eye or that it should be gouged out. Neither does the *right hand* mean our right hand or that it should be cut off. Yet we cannot know what it does mean unless we know what *eye* is a symbol of (specifically the *right eye*), what *hand* is a symbol of (specifically the *right hand*), and what *to cause to sin* means; and we cannot understand what any of these things symbolize, except from the inner meaning.

[6] Cravings are the impulses that come from an evil will and therefore from an evil heart; and as the Lord says in Matthew 15:19, from the will and therefore from the heart come *murders, adulteries, fornications, thefts, false testimonies*—the very impulses covered in the previous commandments. This is why *you shall not covet what belongs to your neighbor* stands for watching out so that the wicked notions covered in the preceding commandments do not become part of our will and then come out in our actions. It also stands for watching out for self-love and worldly ambition, because all the evil we crave gushes, so to speak, from these two sources.

8911. What has been said so far describes our condition in life. Our character is determined by our will, and this character survives after death—death not being the end of life but an extension of it. Our character is dependent on our will, because—as we have already established—our will is who we really are. On this account, being judged by our actions is equivalent to being judged according to our will. Our will and our behavior do not disagree; within our will is our behavior, and within our behavior is our will. But this is the case only as long as we are not held back by such external bonds as fear of the law or fear of the loss of respect, of our wealth, of our reputation, or of our life.

It works like impulse and motion. Motion is nothing more than an extension of the impulse, since the motion stops when the impulse stops. There is nothing essential within the motion except the impulse. Educated people know this, as it is a recognized and proven theory. Because impulse and motion are alive within us, let us put it in terms of human life: the impulse is our will, and the motion is our behavior.

Being judged according to our will is the same as being judged according to what we love, to our life goals, or to the life we lead. Our will is what we love, what we live for, and actually our life itself. The Lord's words cited in the previous passage demonstrate that this is the case: *everyone who looks at a woman with lust has already committed adultery with her in his heart.*

Killing someone is not just doing the deed but wanting to do it, symbolized in Matthew 5:22 by *being angry . . . and insulting a brother or sister.* We are also judged by our actions but only to the extent and to the degree that our actions were done as an act of will.

8912. I should briefly explain the inner meaning of the things enumerated in this commandment—the house, the wife, the male servant, the female servant, the ox, the donkey—that we are not supposed to covet. They are the totality of the good and true things that we should believe in. They are not to be taken away from anyone and should not be weakened.

In their inner meaning, these are the very things symbolized by *keep the sabbath holy, honor your father and mother, do not kill, do not commit adultery, do not steal, do not testify as a lying witness.* In the previous sections, we demonstrated that their inner meaning relates entirely to what we should love and what we should believe.

House means anything good, in a general sense. *Wife* means anything true, in a general sense. *Male servant* means passion for spiritual truth; *female servant* means passion for spiritual goodness; *ox* means passion for goodness on an earthly level; and *donkey* means passion for truth on an earthly level. These are what we should not covet, that is, what we should not take away from anyone or weaken in them.

The reason they have this inner meaning is that the inner meaning of the Word exists for the benefit of those in heaven. People in heaven do not comprehend the Word in earthly terms but instead do so in spiritual terms. They do not see *house, wife, male servant, female servant, ox*, and *donkey*. They see the spiritual equivalents, which are the good and true things we should believe in. In other words, the superficial, or literal, meaning is for people in this world; and the inner meaning is for people in heaven. The inner meaning is, however, also for people in this world who are at the same time in heaven, that is, who have goodwill and faith.

—◦—

Revelation Explained (1758–59)

Leading a Life According to the Commandments

948. [4] To be a religious person, one must live by the divine rules that are summarized in the Ten Commandments. Those who do not do this cannot be religious, since they do not respect God, much less love him, and do not respect other people, much less love them. Can a person who steals, commits adultery, murders, or gives false testimony love God or love other people?

Still, anyone can live according to these rules. If we are wise, we do it to be good citizens, to be moral people, and to get along in society; but because they are divine rules, we cannot be saved unless we live according to them for spiritual reasons. We can live by divine commandments in our civic life merely for the sake of the law and the need to avoid worldly punishment. As moral people, we can do so merely to avoid a loss of respect or damage to our reputation and prestige. In fact, we can do so socially because we want to be considered civilized and avoid a reputation for being unreasonable.

Civil law, moral codes, and social codes all dictate that we should not steal, commit adultery, murder, or give false testimony. But avoiding such wrongdoing only because of these codes or laws cannot save us unless we are also doing it because it is spiritual law, in which case we are avoiding wrongdoing because it is sin. People who do this are religious, believing that there is a God, there is a heaven and hell, and there is a life after death. To be sure, they are also good citizens and behave morally and socially: they are good citizens because of the law, they behave morally to earn respect, and they behave socially because it is considered civilized.

Yet if we do not live by these commandments for spiritual reasons, we are neither behaving as a good citizen, behaving morally, nor behaving socially; that is, we are not law-abiding, not respectable, and in fact not civilized, since the divine element is missing. Goodness does not exist or accomplish anything unless it is something that comes from God. Likewise, just behavior, real respectability, and real civility do not exist or accomplish anything unless they come from God, that is, unless they have that divine element in them.

Imagine, if you can, a person who has hell in them—that is, a devil—obeying the law for the law's sake or for the sake of justice and behaving honorably or in any truly human fashion! Real humanity is the consequence of order, that is, of behaving in an orderly way, and it is the consequence of sound reason. God *is* order, and sound reason *comes from* God. In other words, a person who does not avoid wrongdoing because it is sin is not human.

Anyone who obeys these divine commandments as a matter of religion becomes a citizen and inhabitant of heaven. Anyone who does not—even though living outwardly by these commandments according to social expectations, moral codes, and civil law—may become a citizen and inhabitant of this world but not of heaven.

[5] Most cultures know these commandments and obey them because of their religion; that is, they live according to

them because this is what God wants and has commanded them to do. In this way, they communicate with heaven, are connected with God, and so are saved. On the other hand, most people in the Christian world today obey the commandments not because of their religion; they do it to preserve their standing as good citizens and moral people. They do not commit fraud or make money in underhanded ways (at least to the point where they could be caught doing it), commit adultery, blatantly attack people out of revenge or a grudge, or give false testimony. Yet the reason they do not do so is not because these things are sins or offenses against God but because they are worried about jeopardizing their lifestyle, their reputation, their job, their business arrangements, the things they own, their public respect and wealth, or their personal pleasures. If these restraints were not holding them back, they would engage in those acts. Because of this, they do not establish communication with heaven or a partnership with God but only communication with this world and a partnership with themselves. They cannot be saved.

Think about it: if these kinds of outer restraints were removed from you, which happens to everyone after they die, and if those inner restraints—the respect and love for God (which is what religion is)—were not curbing and holding you back, would you not, like a devil, rush into all sorts of theft, adultery, violence, dishonesty, and lustful behavior because you love it and enjoy it? This is what happens. I have experienced it with my own eyes and ears.

949. [3] To the extent we remove what is bad in us because it is sin, goodness flows in and we are able do good from then on, although we are not doing it on our own; it is being done by the Lord.

First, to the extent we do not worship other gods, which also means not loving ourselves or our worldly ambition more than everything else, the Lord replaces these evils with an acknowledgment of God. So now we are not worshipping God from our own means; the ability to worship is a gift from the Lord.

Second, to the extent we do not profane God's name, which also means avoiding the desires that come from self-love and worldly ambition, we love the holy things in the Word and the church. *The name of God* means the holy things in the Word and the church, which are profaned by the desires that come from self-love and worldly ambition.

Third, to the extent we avoid theft, which also means fraud and making money in underhanded ways, sincerity and justice replace it. We love sincerity and justice by being sincere and just, and then we are not acting sincere and just on our own; it is being done by the Lord.

Fourth, to the extent we avoid adultery, which also means unchaste and impure thoughts, marriage love replaces it. This love is the inmost love of heaven, and chastity is at its core.

Fifth, to the extent we avoid murder, which also means grudges and vengeance, which breed violence, the Lord replaces it with his mercy and love.

Sixth, to the extent we avoid false testimony, which also means lies and slander, the Lord replaces it with truthfulness.

Seventh, to the extent we avoid longing for other people's houses, which also means a desire and yearning to own all their possessions, the Lord replaces it with goodwill toward them.

Eighth, to the extent we avoid coveting another's wife, servant, and so forth, love for the Lord takes its place. This also means avoiding our desire and longing to control other people, because the things listed in this commandment refer to a person's values.

These eight commandments contain evil things that should not be done. The two others, however, the third and fourth, involve certain things that *should* be done, namely keeping the Sabbath day holy and honoring one's parents. How these two commandments should be understood, not as people of the Jewish church understood them but as people of the Christian church should understand them, will be explained later.

※ ※ ※

The First Commandment
You Shall Not Make Other Gods for Yourselves

950. [3] *Not making other gods for yourself* also includes not loving yourself and worldly ambition more than anything else. Whatever you love more than anything else, that is your god.

There are pairs of love that are totally opposite to each other: loving yourself versus loving God, and loving the world versus loving heaven. People who love themselves are self-centered. They love evil in all its variety because self-centeredness is nothing but evil, and those who love evil hate good; they even hate God.

People who love themselves above all else submerge their feelings and thoughts in their body and become self-centered, and they are unable to be lifted up by the Lord. When such people are submerged in their body, or they are being self-centered, they think only corporeal thoughts and enjoy only bodily pleasures. They are in the dark about anything beyond that, while the person who is lifted up by the Lord is in the light. Those who are not in the light of heaven but in darkness deny God because they see no evidence of him. They claim that nature is God, some person is God, or some statue is God; they even aspire to be worshipped as gods themselves.

It makes sense, therefore, that people who love themselves above everything else are *worshipping other gods*. Likewise, people whose worldly ambition supersedes all else are worshipping other gods, although to a lesser degree because it is not possible to love the world as much as you love yourself. Self-centered people only love the world because the world serves their own self-interest.

Loving yourself essentially means wanting to control other people simply to enjoy controlling them and to establish your superiority, not to enjoy being useful or for the sake of the public good. Worldly ambition basically means the desire to possess worldly wealth purely to own it and be rich but not to enjoy its usefulness or the good it can do. Both kinds of desire are limitless; if you give them the chance, they gush out infinitely.

⚜ ⚜ ⚜

951. [8] In this world, no one believes that the desire to control people simply for the pleasure of controlling them or wanting to own things simply for the pleasure of owning them and not for enjoying their usefulness harbor within them every kind of evil, including a contempt for and rejection of everything that relates to heaven and the church. When we anticipate being applauded for our beneficence or when we expect a reward, our self-love and worldly ambition are stimulated to do good things for the church, the country, the community, and our neighbor. Therefore, many people consider this desire to be the main motivator in life—what gives us the incentive to achieve great things. It is important to know, however, that these twin desires are valuable to the extent we view usefulness as most important and ourselves as secondary; but they are bad to the extent we view ourselves as most important and usefulness as secondary. In the latter case, we act entirely out of self-interest and on our own; at the center of everything we do is ourself and our self-interest, which seen in isolation is nothing but evil.

On the other hand, focusing on the service to be performed first and ourselves second is doing good for the sake of the church, the country, the community, and other individuals. The good we are doing for them is for their sake, and we are not doing it on our own; it is being done by the Lord. The difference between the two is like the difference between heaven and hell. People do not know there is a difference between the two because they engage in those twin desires from the time they are born, and they cherish and nurture the pleasure they get from them.

[9] Nonetheless, we should recognize that wanting to control others simply for the pleasure of control and not for the joy of being useful is an entirely diabolical desire. It can also be called an atheistic desire because to the extent people indulge in it, in their heart they do not believe God exists, and likewise in their heart they mock anything related to the church. In fact, they hate and angrily attack everyone who acknowledges God, especially anyone who acknowledges the Lord [Jesus Christ].

The life's passion of these people is wrongdoing—committing every sort of wicked and shameful act. In a word, they are actually devils. We are not aware of this while living in this world but will find out upon arrival in the spiritual world, right after we die. Hell is full of people like this, but instead of dominating other people, they are placed into their service. Viewed in the light of heaven, they appear to be upside down—with their head pointing down and their feet up, since their desire to be in charge was most important to them and their desire to be of service secondary. Whatever is most important is our head, and whatever is secondary is our feet; whatever is our head we love, but whatever is our feet we trample on.

⚡ ⚡ ⚡

952. [2] People are fooling themselves if they think they are open to believing that there is a God before they stop doing the evil things listed in the Ten Commandments. This is especially true of wanting to control other people for the pleasure of controlling them and wanting to own worldly things for the pleasure of owning them but not wanting these things for the pleasure of doing something useful. Such people can reassure themselves as much as they want that there is a God—from the Word, from sermons, from books, from common sense—and convince themselves that they believe it, but in fact they do not believe it unless the evil pouring out of their self-love and worldly ambition is removed. This is because evil, and the pleasure that comes with it, gets in the way of heaven's goodness, diverts it, and pushes it away along with the ability to enjoy it. In this way, it prevents them from confirming their belief.

Until heaven strengthens our belief, it is only professed belief, which is no belief at all. It is not heartfelt belief, which is real belief. Professed belief is putting our trust in outer restraint, but heartfelt belief is putting our trust in inner restraint. When inner restraint has become jammed up with all kinds of evil, and then our outer restraint is taken away (which happens to everyone after death), that evil then causes us to reject our belief in God.

⚡ ⚡ ⚡

954. [2] We must resist these twin selfish desires: wanting to control people purely for the pleasure of controlling them and wanting to own things purely for the pleasure of owning them. To the extent we avoid them, and also avoid the evils listed in the Ten Commandments as sins, the belief in God who is the creator and guardian of the universe (and in fact is one God) flows into us from the Lord through heaven. This belief flows into us because heaven is opened up when evil is removed; and when heaven is opened up, we are no longer thinking on our own—our thought is coming from the Lord through heaven. This idea that there is a God and that he is one is the universal concept in heaven, encompassing all others.

The common belief of people around the world and the difficulty they have conceiving of multiple gods prove that simply from heavenly influence we can know or, so to speak, see that there is one God. Our inner thought, the thought of our spirit, comes either from hell or from heaven. It is from hell until evils have been removed, but as long as they are removed, it is from heaven. When someone's inner thought comes from hell, that person reckons only that nature is God and that what we call divine is just the underlying mechanics of nature. After they die and become spirits, people like this say that whoever is the mightiest is a god, and then they claim they themselves are powerful so that they can be called a god. This madness lurks within every evil compulsion in their spirit.

But when our thought is from heaven, which happens as long as evil is removed, we see in the light of heaven that there is a God and that he is one. Seeing in the light of heaven is what I mean by heavenly influence.

⚜ ⚜ ⚜

955. [4] When we avoid and reject wrongdoing because it is sin, not only do we see in heavenly light that there is a God and that he is one, but we also see God as a person. This is because we want to see our God, and we cannot see him other than as a person. This is how the ancient peoples before and after the time of Abraham saw God. This is how people all over the world who are not in the church see him intuitively—especially those who, although uneducated, have an inner wisdom. This is how all babies and children see him, as well as those who are simple, decent folk. This is also how people from other planets see God; they say that what is invisible cannot be a part of their faith, since they cannot picture it.

The reason such people see God as a human being is because those who avoid and reject wrongdoing as sin are thinking from heaven, and the whole of heaven—and each individual there—pictures God as a human being. No other image is possible, since the whole of heaven is in the shape of an immense human being, and also since the divine quality that flows forth from the Lord is what makes up heaven. It is impossible for angels to think about God as having anything other than that divine form, which is the human form, and the angels fill up heaven with their thoughts about it. In *Heaven and Hell* 51–86, read about how all of heaven taken together relates to the human form; and in *Heaven and Hell* 200–212, read about how the angels think in accordance with the form of heaven.

[5] This image of God flows from heaven into everyone in this world, and it resides in their spirit. For those in the church who rely on their own intelligence, the image of God seems to have been expunged; it has been expunged [in such a way] as to be inconceivable, because they are thinking about God in spatial terms. These same people see it quite differently when they become spirits, as I have experienced frequently. In the spiritual world, an indeterminate picture of God is no picture at all, so they are provided a definite image of someone sitting on high, or someplace special, and responding to their petitions.

From the general influence of the spiritual world, people get an image of God as a human being, varying according to their perceptive ability. This is why the threefold God is referred to as *persons* and why in our churches God the Father is depicted as an old man. This general influence of the spiritual world is also why the human beings known as saints—both living and dead—are worshipped as gods by the common folk in the Christian world and why statues of the saints are venerated by them. This is likewise the case among many non-Christians in other parts of the world as well as among the people of ancient Greece, Rome, and Asia, who had many gods and pictured them as humans.

I have said all this so you can know that the ability to see God as a human being is instinctive in the human spirit. When I say *instinctive*, I mean it comes from that general influence of the spiritual world.

956. [2] If people who are in their spirit can see God as a human being on account of this general influence of heaven, it makes sense that those who are in a religion that has the Word can see that the Lord's divine nature is within his human manifestation, that the Trinity is within him, and that he himself is the God of heaven and earth. They can see these things as long as they avoid and reject wrongdoing as sin, because then they are in heavenly light.

On the other hand, those who have impaired their concept of God as a human being by thinking from a selfish point of view are unable to see this. Nor are they able to see that God is one, because they are thinking of a Trinity while publicly saying there is only one God.

Furthermore, people who have not been cleansed of wrongdoing are not in heavenly light and cannot see in their spirit that the Lord is the God of heaven and earth. They see something else in his place: some see a being whom they believe to be God the Father; some see a being whom they call God because he is all-powerful; some see a devil whom they fear because he is extremely dangerous; some see nature, as do many in this world; and some see no God at all. *In their spirit* refers to the way people are when they die and become spirits. Whatever lies hidden in their spirit in this world is disclosed at that point.

Every person in heaven without exception acknowledges only the Lord. Heaven derives entirely from the divine quality that comes from him, and it mirrors him in his human form. None can enter heaven unless they are within the Lord, because they enter him when they enter heaven. If any others enter heaven, they cease to function mentally and fall back down.

⚜ ⚜ ⚜

957. [3] Our concept of God is the most important concept of all. The quality of our concept of God determines our level of communication with heaven and our connection with the Lord, and it therefore determines our level of enlightenment, our passion for what is true and good, our inner perception, and our intelligence and wisdom. These faculties do not come from us; they come from the Lord, depending on how connected we are with him.

The correct concept of God is a concept of the Lord and his divine nature, because the Lord is nothing other than the God of heaven and the God of earth, as he teaches us in Matthew 28:18: "All authority in heaven and on earth has been given to me."

However, one's concept of the Lord can be more or less complete, more or less precise. The concept is complete in the innermost heaven, less complete in the middle heaven, and even less complete in the outer heaven; and accordingly, people in the innermost heaven are *wise*, those in the middle heaven are merely *intelligent*, and those in the outer heaven are merely *knowledgeable*. The concept is precise for angels who are in the midst of their communities in heaven and less precise for those who are round about, depending on how far they are from the center.

[4] People in heaven are allotted a place to live according to how complete and precise their concept of the Lord is, and they are granted a level of wisdom and happiness accordingly. People who have no conception of the Lord being divine, such as the Socinians and the Arians, live beneath the heavens and are unhappy. People who have a dual concept, namely an invisible god *and* a visible god in human form, also reside beneath the heavens and are not allowed in until they accept that there is one God and that he is visible.

Because God is called a spirit, some see something airy instead of a visible God. They are not accepted in heaven until this changes into the concept of a human being, that is, of the Lord. Certain ones who have a concept of God as being the underlying mechanics of nature are rejected because they cannot help but lapse into the idea that nature is God.

Any of the non-Christian peoples in the world who have believed in one God and thought of him as a human being are received into heaven by the Lord. The point of all this is that there are people who worship one God and people who worship multiple gods—in other words, those who live according to the first commandment and those who do not.

The Second Commandment
You Shall Not Profane the Name of God

959. [2] I will first explain what *the name of God* means and then what it means to *profane the name of God*.

The name of God means every characteristic we worship in God. God has, and is, his own character. His essence is divine love, and therefore his character is the divine truth united with divine goodness. For us on earth, that is the Word, as it says in John 1:1: "The Word was with God, and the Word was God."

This is where the teaching about what is really true and good in the Word comes from, which is the basis of worship.

[3] God's character is multifaceted because it includes all the things that he does. Therefore, he has many names, each name incorporating and describing his character in both a general and specific way. For example, he is called *Jehovah, Jehovah Zebaoth, Lord, Lord Jehovih, God, Messiah* or *Christ, Jesus, Savior, Redeemer, Creator, Shaper, Maker, King, Holy One of Israel, Rock* and *Stone of Israel, Shiloh, Shaddai, David, Prophet, Son of God,* and *Son of Man,* and many more besides. All these names are the names for one God, who is the Lord; yet when they are mentioned in the Word, they refer to a certain overall divine attribute or characteristic as distinguished from separate, individual divine attributes or characteristics. Likewise, when *Father, Son, and Holy Spirit* are mentioned we should not think of three gods but instead should think of one. Nor are there three divine beings; there is one. This threefold God, who is one, is the Lord.

[4] Each name stands for some distinct attribute or characteristic, and therefore *profaning the name of God* does not mean profaning his *name* but instead his *character.* A name stands for one's character, because in heaven all are named for their character. God's character, or the Lord's character, is everything that comes from him and that we worship in him. This is why they are unable to name the Lord in hell, where they do not recognize the Lord as having any divine characteristic. It is also why his names cannot be uttered by

anyone in the spiritual world unless his divine characteristic is recognized, since everyone there speaks from the heart, that is, from love and the recognition that comes from love.

⚜ ⚜ ⚜

960. [14] *The name of God* means what comes from God, or what he is. This is called the divine truth, or, by us on earth, the Word. The Word is not to be profaned, because it is divinity itself and is most holy. We profane the Word when we deny its holiness by having contempt for it, rejecting it, or being ashamed of it. When we do this, heaven is closed off and we are relegated to hell. The Word is the only means of connecting heaven with the church; so when people reject the Word in their heart, that connection with heaven is broken and, being relegated to hell, they no longer accept any of the truth taught by the church.

[15] There are two ways heaven can be closed off to people: one is by denying that the Lord is divine, and the other is by denying that the Word is holy. This is because the whole essence of heaven is the Lord's divinity and because the divine truth (the Word in its spiritual meaning) organizes heaven. So it makes sense that people who deny the one or the other are denying either that which is the whole essence of heaven or that by which heaven functions. In this way, those people are cutting off communication and connection with heaven.

Profaning the Word is the same as blaspheming the Holy Spirit, for which no one is forgiven. This is why this commandment says, *whoever profanes the name of God will not remain unpunished.*

⚜ ⚜ ⚜

962. [11] We profane the name of God inwardly when we live contrary to the requirements in the Ten Commandments, because *the name of God* means divine truth, or the Word, and profaning it means denying the Word's holiness, having contempt for it, rejecting it, and blaspheming it.

Profanation can either be inward but not at the same time outward, or it can be inward and outward at the same time, or there can even be some profanation outwardly without inward profanation occurring at the same time.

We profane inwardly by how we live and outwardly by what we say. After death, the inward profanation that is based on how we live also becomes outward, or spoken, profanation. After we die, we all speak and act according to the thoughts and desires of our daily life, to the extent we are allowed. This is not what we do in this world, where, on account of worldly ambition and building our reputation, we are accustomed to speak and act differently from our everyday thoughts and desires. Therefore, we can be said to profane inwardly without at the same time profaning outwardly.

The way the Word is written, not at all in an earthly style, leaves open the possibility of some outward profanation without inward profanation. It is possible to have a certain amount of contempt for the Word if its inner holiness is not recognized.

✦ ✦ ✦

963. [2] When we resist profaning the name of God, that is, the holiness of the Word—not having contempt for it, rejecting it, or blaspheming it in any way—we are being religious. We are being religious only to the extent we resist this profanation, since no one has religion unless it comes from revelation, and for us that means the Word.

We must from our heart, not only with our mouth, resist profaning the Word's holiness. Those who do it from the heart are leading religious lives. Those who do it only with their mouth are not leading religious lives. They are resisting either for selfish or worldly reasons. The Word is serving them only as a means to enhance their reputation and their wealth, or they are doing it out of fear. Most of these are hypocrites, and they have no religion.

⚜ ⚜ ⚜

The Third Commandment
Keep the Sabbath Holy

965. [2] The third and fourth commandments cover the things we *should* do (keep the Sabbath holy and honor our parents), while the other commandments are about what we *should not* do: worship other gods, profane the name of God, steal, commit adultery, give false testimony, and long for what other people have. The reason these two are commandments that *should* be done is because the ability of the other commandments to make us holy depends on them.

The Sabbath represents the union within the Lord of his underlying divine nature and his deified human aspect, and consequently it represents the Lord's connection with heaven and the church. Ultimately, it represents the marriage of goodness and truth in a person who is being regenerated. Because the Sabbath used to stand for those things, it was the most important symbol of all aspects of worship in the Israelite Church, as is obvious in Jeremiah (17:20–27 and other passages). It was the primary symbol of all aspects of worship, because the most important aspect of worship is acknowledging the Lord's divine nature within his human manifestation. If we do not acknowledge that, we cannot help but rely on our own faith and actions. Relying on our own faith means believing false things, and relying on our own actions means doing evil things, which is obvious from the Lord's own words in John:

Then they said to him, "What must we do to perform the works of God?" Jesus answered them, "This is the work of God, that you believe in him whom he has sent." (John 6:28–29)

Again in John,

Those who abide in me and I in them bear much fruit, because apart from me you can do nothing. (John 15:5)

⚜ ⚜ ⚜

The Fourth Commandment
Parents Should Be Honored

966. [2] We were given this commandment because honoring parents symbolized, and therefore meant, loving the Lord and the church. The heavenly meaning of *father* is the Lord: he is our heavenly Father. The heavenly meaning of *mother* is the church: it is our heavenly Mother. *Honor* symbolizes wanting to do what is right, and *prolonging the days* of those who want to do what is right symbolizes the happiness of eternal life.

This is how the commandment is understood in heaven, where they recognize no other father than the Lord and no other mother than the Lord's kingdom, which is the church. The Lord gives us life from himself, and he nurtures us through the church.

The Lord teaches us in Matthew the heavenly meaning of this commandment, which is that while we are in a heavenly state of mind we should not think of, or even mention, an earthly father:

And call no one your father on earth, for you have one Father—the one in heaven. (Matthew 23:9)

. . . These explanations demonstrate how the third and fourth commandments veil mysteries about the Lord, namely, accepting and affirming that he is divine and worshipping him by wanting to do what is right.

The Fifth Commandment
You Shall Not Steal

967. [3] *Stealing* here does not just mean blatant stealing. It also means subtle forms of stealing like usury or taking advantage of people by various types of fraud or cunning, which either look legal or are done secretly so that no one knows. This sort of exploitation may be engaged in by money managers of large and small accounts, by businessmen, or by judges who make justice a commodity by selling their decisions.

These and many others are examples of theft, and we are to resist them and avoid them. Ultimately, we should reject them because they are sins against God, since they are against the divine laws in the Word and against this specific law, which is one of the fundamental laws of all religions throughout the world. These Ten Commandments are universal, given to us so that we may live according to religion by living according to them. Living according to religion connects people to heaven, whereas living only in obedience to the civil and moral law connects them to this world but not heaven. Being connected to this world and not heaven is the same as being connected to hell.

969. [2] Each one of us is created to be an image of heaven and an image of the world, because everyone is a microcosm. We are born an image of the world from our parents, and we are reborn to be an image of heaven. To be reborn is to be regenerated, and we are regenerated by the Lord through the truth in the Word and through our living according to that truth.

We are images of the world with respect to our earthly mind, and we are images of heaven with respect to our spiritual mind. Our earthly mind *is* this world and is in the lower position. Our spiritual mind is heaven and is above our earthly mind. Our earthly mind is full of every kind of wickedness: theft, adultery, murder, false witness, cravings, even blasphemy and profanity against God. These wicked impulses, and many more besides, inhabit our earthly mind because it is in that mind that we love these wicked things; and so we enjoy thinking about them, enjoy yearning for them, and enjoy doing them. We inherit from our parents these impulses in our earthly mind, where we are born into them and grow up into them. Only the constraints of civil law or of a moral code prevent people from doing these things and from revealing, therefore, the compulsions of their depraved will.

[3] Who cannot see that the Lord is unable to flow into us from heaven and teach and lead us until this wickedness has been removed? It obstructs, repels, deflects, and smothers the good and true things from heaven that are persistently trying to settle down upon us, and eventually flow into us, from above. Wicked things are hellish, and good things are heavenly; and everything hellish burns with hatred against anything heavenly. In consequence of this, the pile of wickedness that has accumulated in our earthly mind needs to be removed before the Lord can flow in from and with heaven and shape us into an image of heaven.

The reason why eight of the Ten Commandments spell out wicked deeds that *should not* be done, and not good deeds that *should* be done, is that the removal of wickedness must happen first before a person can be taught and led by the Lord. Something good comes about neither in the presence of something wicked nor before that wickedness is removed. Until that happens, there is no pathway from heaven into us. We are like a dark sea whose waters must be pushed away on either side before the Lord in his cloud and fire can provide a crossing for the children of Israel. In fact, *dark sea* symbolizes hell, *Pharaoh with his Egyptians* symbolizes our earthly self, and the *children of Israel* symbolize our spiritual self.

⚜ ⚜ ⚜

970. [2] As I said before, there is no communication with heaven until the evil (and consequent falsehood) clogging up our earthly mind has been removed. This falsehood is like dark clouds lying between the sun and our eyes. Or, it is like a wall that stands between the light of heaven and the light of a candle in a cell: As long as we are only illuminated on the earthly plane, we are like a person shut up in that cell and seeing by candlelight. Yet as soon as we have been purified of evil (and the consequent falsity) on the earthly plane, it is like looking through windows in the wall—windows to heaven— with the light of heaven shining through them.

Our higher mind, the spiritual mind, is opened as soon as evil has been removed. The image of heaven is essentially imprinted on this mind, and the Lord flows in through our spiritual mind and makes it so we can see in the light of heaven. It is also through this mind that he reforms and ultimately regenerates us on the earthly plane, replacing falsehood with truth, and evil with goodness. The Lord accomplishes this by means of spiritual love, the love of what is good and true. At this point we are positioned midway between dual desires: wanting what is evil and wanting what is good. When our desire for evil subsides, a desire for goodness replaces it. Our desire for evil only subsides when we live according to the Ten Commandments, resisting because they are sins the wicked acts spelled out there and ultimately fleeing from them as something infernal.

[3] In short, as long as we do not resist evil because it is sin, our spiritual mind is closed. But the moment we resist evil as sin, our spiritual mind is opened and with it heaven. Once heaven is opened, we see everything in a different light involving the church, heaven, and eternal life. While we are living in this world, we hardly notice the difference between this new light and the old. This is because a person in this world thinks even about spiritual things from an earthly point of view, and spiritual ideas are wrapped in earthly ideas up to the point of crossing over from this earthly world into the spiritual world. In the spiritual world, they are uncovered, are understood, and become obvious.

⚜ ⚜ ⚜

971. [2] Goodness flows into us from the Lord to the degree that we resist wrongdoing and that we avoid it and reject it because it is sin. The goodness that flows into us is a passion for learning and understanding the truth, and it is a passion for wanting to do—and doing—what is right. However, we cannot resist wrongdoing by avoiding it and rejecting it by ourselves, because we have been engaged in evil since we were born and it is in our nature. Evil cannot avoid evil by itself. That would be like us avoiding our own nature, which is impossible. For this reason, it must be the Lord, who is divine goodness and divine truth, who enables us to avoid doing those things. Even so, we should avoid them as though we are doing it ourselves, because whatever we do as though we are doing it on our own we take responsibility for and is credited to us. Whatever we do not do as though we are doing it on our own we never take responsibility for and is not credited to us. We should accept whatever comes to us from the Lord, but we cannot accept it unless we do so consciously, that is, unless we seem to be doing it on our own. This reciprocation is necessary for reformation.

This is why these Ten Commandments were given and why we are ordered in them not to worship other gods; not to profane the name of God; not to steal; not to commit adultery; not to kill; and not to long for the home, the wife, and the servants of other people. This is why we are commanded to stop doing these things even in our thinking—when our desire for evil incites us and tantalizes us—and that they should not be done, because they are sins against God and inherently hellish. To the degree we avoid them, a desire for what is true and good comes into us from the Lord. This desire causes us to avoid and ultimately reject those wicked actions because they are sins. Since it is our desire for truth and goodness that puts these evils to flight, it is obvious that we do not avoid them on our own; it is done by the Lord, because our desire for truth and goodness comes from the Lord. If we avoid doing evil only because we fear hell, the evil is in fact removed, but goodness does not replace it. As soon as the fear goes away, the evil returns.

[3] Only humans are able to think as if independently about right and wrong: to think that one ought to love what is right and do it because it is divine and has eternal consequences, and to hate what is wrong and not do it because it is diabolical and has eternal consequences. No other creature can think this way. An animal is able to do something good and avoid doing something bad, but it cannot do so independently. It is either from instinct, training, or fear, but never from thinking, "this is the right thing, this is the wrong thing"—in other words, not from thinking independently.

Those who claim that we do not avoid evil or do what is right independently but do it instead from a subconscious influence, or by taking credit for what the Lord does, want us to believe that we live without contemplating, understanding, or being inspired by what is good and true, like an animal. Many experiences in the spiritual world have demonstrated to me that we do, in fact, think independently. After death, everyone is prepared there for heaven or hell. Evil is removed from the person being prepared for heaven, and goodness is removed from the person being prepared for hell. In all cases, the removal happens as though the people are doing it themselves. Accordingly, those who do evil things are driven by punishments to reject them as though they were doing so on their own. If it did not happen as though they did it on their own, the punishment would have no effect.

Obviously, those who throw up their hands, waiting to be directed by some influence or waiting to be given credit for the Lord's good works, stay stuck in their own wickedness with their hands in the air forever.

[4] Avoiding wickedness because it is sinful means avoiding the hellish communities that engage in that wickedness. We cannot avoid these communities unless we reject them and turn away from them, and we cannot turn away in opposition unless we love what is good. When we want to do what is right, we have no wish to do wrong. We either choose wrong or choose right, and we choose right to the degree we do not choose what is wrong. The ability to choose what is right comes from obeying the Ten Commandments as a matter of our religion, and it also comes from living according to those commandments.

[5] The Ten Commandments were written by the Lord on matching tablets so that we can refrain from wrongdoing because it is sinful, as though we are doing it on our own. They were called a *covenant* because it was a contract entered into as other contracts between two parties are entered into, where

one party states the arrangement and the other party agrees to it. When we agree to it, we are giving our consent. If we do not consent, the contract does not hold up. Consenting in this case means thinking, wanting, and acting on our own.

Although we think that we are avoiding wickedness and doing what is right on our own, we are not; the Lord is doing it. He does it for the sake of reciprocation, which then results in connection. It is the nature of the Lord's divine love to want us to have what he has, but since he is divine, it cannot be ours, and so he makes it seem as though it is ours. This is how that mutual connection comes about, so that we can be within the Lord and he within us, according to the Lord's own words in John (14:20). This could not happen if we did not seem to play some role in the connection.

Whatever we do as though on our own, we do as though it is our idea. We are enthusiastic about it and we are doing it freely, and in this way we are leading our own lives. If we on our part do not act as though we are doing it ourselves, we would not take responsibility for it because we played no part in it, and therefore there would be no contract and no connection. In fact, we could never be held to account for doing wrong versus right, for believing what is true versus what is false, and consequently we could not go to hell deservedly for evil deeds, or to heaven as a reward for good deeds.

972. [2] When we resist theft in its broadest definition, and in fact flee from it, but for some reason other than religion and eternal life, we are not purified of theft. Heaven is not open to us in any other way [than avoiding evil for the sake of religion and eternal life]. It is through heaven that the Lord removes the evil in us, just as it is through heaven that he removes hell.

Examples of this might be money managers of either large or small accounts, businessmen, judges, public officials of any sort, or workers, who refrain from thefts such as improper charges or fees but do so in the pursuit of a good reputation and the respect and financial reward that come with it or because of civil law or moral expectations. The point is that they are avoiding it out of some earthly desire or fear, that is, not from religion but only from outward constraints. Inside they are still full of theft and avarice, which burst forth whenever these constraints are removed, as happens to everyone after they die. Their sincerity and rectitude is only a mask or a clever ruse.

꙳ ꙳ ꙳

973. [2] To the degree theft has been removed in us, whether theft in general or a particular kind, and to the degree more may be removed in the future, it is replaced by the corresponding positive action, which mainly has to do with being sincere, honest, and just. When we avoid and reject making money illicitly by means of fraud and trickery, to that extent we want what is sincere, honest, and just. Ultimately, we come to love sincerity for the sake of sincerity, honesty for the sake of honesty, and justice for the sake of justice. We come to love them because they are given to us by the Lord and his love is in them. Loving the Lord does not mean loving a visage of him but loving the things that come from him. These are the Lord in us, and so we also have real sincerity, real honesty, and real justice within us. Because these things are what the Lord is, to the extent we love them and act according to them we are acting on the Lord's behalf, and to that extent the Lord removes insincerity and injustice—even their roots, which are the intention and desire to engage in them. Each time we do this, it becomes less of a struggle and a battle, and therefore it takes less effort than it did in the beginning.

By this process, we think from conscience and act with integrity, but we do not do it on our own, only *as though* on our own: we accept (on faith at first and later with understanding) that it seems like we are thinking and acting independently (when in fact we are not doing it on our own) but that it is on the Lord's behalf.

∗ ∗ ∗

974. [2] When we begin to avoid and reject evil because it is sinful, everything we do subsequently is good and can be considered good works depending on how useful they are. Before we avoid and reject evil because it is a sin, all of the things we do are evil. They are our own efforts; they are in our own self-interest and therefore nothing but evil, and we do them merely for worldly reasons. The things we do after avoiding and rejecting evil because it is sin are the Lord's works, because they are in his interest and therefore in heaven's interest.

The difference between works that are done by us and works that are done by the Lord within us is not apparent from a human perspective, but it is fully apparent from the angels' perspective. [From their perspective,] the works we undertake on our own are like tombs that are whitewashed on the outside but contain the bones of the dead within; like the cup and the plate that are clean on the outside but absolutely filthy on the inside; like an apple that is rotten at the core but polished on the outside; like nuts or almonds that are eaten out by worms, though the shell is still intact; or like a diseased prostitute with a beautiful face. That is what it is like when we undertake works on our own. However good they may appear on the outside, on the inside those endeavors are brimming with impurities of every kind; their interior is hellish while their exterior seems heavenly.

On the other hand, after we avoid and reject evil because it is sin, the works we undertake are not only good on the outside but good on the inside as well. They become better and better the deeper you go, because the deeper you go, the closer you are to the Lord. Then our endeavors are like fruit with delicious flesh, and at the core is a seed pod producing enough new trees to fill orchards. All the individual particles in our earthly being become like eggs that hatch out endless flocks of birds that fill the whole sky.

To put it briefly, so long as we avoid and oppose evil because it is sin, the endeavors we undertake are alive; those we undertook previously were dead. Whatever comes from the Lord is alive, but whatever comes from us is dead.

❖　❖　❖

975. [2] I have stated that we do good to the extent we avoid and reject what is bad because they are sins; that this good is the good works referred to in the Word because they are happening within the Lord; and also that these efforts are good to the extent we reject the evil works contrary to them, because to that extent they are being done by the Lord and not by us. Our works are, however, more or less good depending on how useful they are, since by definition good works must be useful. The best works are ones that are of use to the church, the next in goodness are works that are useful to our country, and so on. Usefulness determines how good our works are.

The goodness of our endeavors increases with the fullness of the truth by which we are inspired to perform them. People who reject evil because it is sin want to know the truth, because truth teaches them what is useful about those works and why they are good. This is why goodness loves truth and truth loves goodness, and this is why they want to be joined together. When such people learn truth because they are inspired by it, they do good things with greater wisdom and depth: with greater wisdom because they are learning what is useful and how to do it with good judgment and a sense of justice; and with greater depth because all of that truth is present in the performance of these useful activities, and when we are inspired by truth, it creates a spiritual climate around us.

⚜ ⚜ ⚜

976. [2] Take judges, for example: all those judges who consider justice a commodity to be bought and sold, loving their position for the money they can make off the rulings they render and not for the service they provide to their country, are thieves; and their rulings are thefts. It is the same if they make judgments on the basis of friendship or favoritism, which are a form of profit and payment. As long as they have these as their goal and their judgments as the means, every judicial action they take is evil. In the Word, these actions are referred to as *evil works* and *not acting with justice and judgment, violating the rights of the poor, the needy, orphans, widows, and the innocent.*

Even if they do dispense justice, they may indeed be doing a good deed; but as long as they have personal gain as their goal, it is not for the benefit of their petitioners. Justice, which is divine, is a means for them, but their goal is personal gain. What we have as our goal is everything to us, but whatever we have as our means is nothing except to the extent it serves our goal.

After death, judges of this sort value justice no more than they do injustice, and they are condemned to hell as thieves. I speak from experience on this. These are people who resist evil not because it is a sin but only out of fear of the civil law or of losing their reputation, their recognition, their position, and the money they get from it.

[3] The case is very different with judges who resist evil because it is sin and avoid it because it is contrary to divine law and so contrary to God. These judges have justice as their goal; and they revere, worship, and love it as something divine. It is as though they see God in justice, because everything that is just comes from God, as all good and true things do. They always equate what is legally right with fairness and fairness with what is legally right. They believe that in order for something to be lawful it must be fair, and in order for it to be fair it must be lawful—just as something true must be good, and something good must be true.

Since they have justice as their goal, in their minds rendering rulings is the same as doing good works. In their view, these works—their rulings—are more or less good depending on how much they take friendship, favoritism, and personal gain into account. Accordingly, they consider their rulings more or less good depending on how much they bring to bear a love of justice for the sake of the public welfare. In this way, they ensure that justice prevails among their fellow citizens and that those who abide by the law can live in safety. These judges live eternally in a standing commensurate with their works: they are judged as they have judged.

⚜ ⚜ ⚜

977. [2] Take, for example, money managers of accounts large or small: if they embezzle from their rulers, the government, or their employers, either skimming money secretly or engaging in open fraud, they are not religious people and have no conscience. They are scorning the divine law against theft and acting as though it is nothing. They may attend church frequently, listen attentively to all the sermons, take the holy supper, pray morning and evening, and quote piously from the Word; but still nothing can flow from heaven into their worship, their piety, and their speech, because inside they are full of theft, plunder, robbery, and injustice. As long as these things are inside them, the channel from heaven is closed off. Consequently, all the works they undertake are evil.

[3] On the other hand, money managers who avoid illicit profit and fraudulent income because it is contrary to the divine law against theft are religious people and are therefore conscientious. Their works are all good because they do them sincerely and justly on account of the divine law against theft. Furthermore, they are content with what they have and are happy in heart and mind whenever there is an opportunity not to commit fraud. When they die, they are taken up by the angels, who receive them as friends and bestow wealth upon them to the point of affluence.

It is quite the reverse with evil money managers. When they die, they are banished from society, become beggars, and end up being put to work in a den of thieves.

⚜ ⚜ ⚜

978. [2] For another example, consider merchants: even if they are not engaging in improper business practices, usury, frauds, and scams, as long as they are not trying to avoid these things because they are sins, all their works are wicked. Such actions cannot come from the Lord but only from the merchants themselves.

Their actions are all the worse when they learn how to perfect well-practiced and glib sales pitches and string their customers along; and worse still are their actions when they learn how to make the sale under the impression that they are being sincere, just, and devout. The more delight a merchant takes in this, the more his actions originate in hell.

Suppose these merchants act sincerely and justly to earn a good reputation so they can get rich. It seems like they want to be sincere and just, and yet they are not acting sincerely and justly because they want to or out of obedience to divine law. Inside, they are being insincere and unjust, and their actions constitute theft because they want to steal by pretending to be sincere and just.

[3] This is exposed after death, when people act on their inner wants and desires instead of their apparent wants and desires. After they die, merchants of this sort do nothing but dream up ways to carry out elaborate burglaries. They sneak away from honest folk and find their way into the woods or deserted areas to scheme. In a word, they become robbers.

It is completely otherwise for merchants who have avoided every sort of theft because it is a sin, especially the inward and more hidden kind of theft accomplished by trickery and deception. All their works are good works because they are done on the Lord's behalf. The heavenly influence (from the Lord through heaven) that leads them to undertake good works has not been blocked by the kind of wrongdoing just described.

These merchants are not harmed by wealth. For them, wealth is a means of doing useful things, and useful activity for them is a business in which they can be of service to their country and their fellow citizens. Their wealth puts them in a position to do the useful things to which they are inclined by their passion for doing good.

✣ ✣ ✣

979. [2] Based on what I have said so far, it is obvious what *good works* in the Word means. It means any effort we undertake so long as evil has been removed because it is sin. Whatever we do at that point is not being done by us; it is being done *as though* we are doing it. The deeds are being done by the Lord, and whatever he does is good—whether you call it leading a good life, being charitable, or doing good works.

In the same way, every ruling rendered by a judge is good when the judge has justice as the goal, celebrates and loves justice as something divine, and detests as shameful rulings that are issued in return for money, for the sake of friendship, or for favoritism. The judge is providing for the good of the country by ensuring that good judgment and justice reign there as they do in heaven, and the judge is providing for a peaceful life for every innocent citizen by protecting them from being harmed by bad people; all of this constitutes good works. The work of money managers and the deals of merchants are all good works when they avoid making money in inappropriate ways because it is a sin contrary to divine laws.

When we avoid evil as sin, every day we learn what good deeds are, and within us grows a passion for doing good things as well as a passion for learning truth so we can do good things. The more we learn the truth, the more deeply and wisely we undertake our endeavors; and as a result, our works become more truly good. And so stop asking yourself, "What good works should I undertake, or what good thing must I do to attain eternal life?" Just resist evil because it is sinful and look to the Lord, and the Lord will teach you and guide you.

❧ ❧ ❧

The Sixth Commandment
You Shall Not Commit Adultery

981. [2] Who these days can believe that the enjoyment of adultery is hell within us; that the enjoyment of marriage is heaven within us; and therefore, to the degree we enjoy the one we cannot enjoy the other, because to the extent a person is in hell they cannot be in heaven?

Who these days can believe that desiring adultery is fundamental to every kind of infernal and diabolical love, and that desiring a faithful marriage is fundamental to every kind of heavenly and divine love? Who can believe that to the extent we want to commit adultery, we want to do every kind of evil—if not actually, at least in intention—and conversely, to the extent we desire a faithful marriage, we want to do everything good—if not actually, at least in intention?

Who these days can believe that people who desire adultery do not believe anything the Word says or anything the church says, and they in fact deny God in their heart; and conversely, that people who desire a faithful marriage have goodwill, are believing, and love God?

Finally, who these days can believe that faithfulness in marriage goes hand in hand with religion, and that adulterous lust goes hand in hand with materialism?

[3] The reason these things are unknown nowadays is because the church is in its end stage, and it is devoid of truth and goodness. When the church is in a state like this, its members can be swayed by hellish influence to believe that adultery is not detestable and abominable. They can come to believe that adultery and marriage are essentially no different from each other, other than marriage preserving order in society, when indeed the difference between them is like that between heaven and hell. In the following section, we will examine the difference between them.

The above propositions explain why in the Word the spiritual meaning of *weddings* and *marriages* is heaven and the church and why *adulteries* and *fornications* mean hell and a rejection of everything the Word says about the church.

* * *

982. [5] Since adultery is hell within us and marriage is heaven within us, we remove ourselves from heaven to the degree we desire adultery. As a result, to the extent we consider adultery allowable and more enjoyable than marriage, adultery closes off heaven and opens up hell. People who justify their own adultery, indulge in it willfully, and oppose marriage close heaven off to themselves to the point that they no longer believe anything the Word or the church says. They become totally sensual, and after they die they become infernal. As I said previously, adultery is hell, and an adulterer is a form of hell.

Because adultery is hell, unless people resist adultery, avoid it, and reject it as infernal, they close heaven off to themselves and do not receive even a tiny bit of its influence. From that point on, they rationalize that adultery and marriage are similar, although they admit that marriage should be protected in society for the sake of order and raising children. They also rationalize that adultery should not be vilified since it can produce children just as well as can marriage, it is not harmful to women because it is a means of support for them, and it advances the procreation of the human race. They do not know that these and similar arguments made in favor of adultery are rationalizations wafting up from the Stygian waters of hell. They also do not know that when we take joy in adultery, the lustful and wild nature inherent in us from birth snatches and sucks in these rationalizations like a hog devouring its slop.

You will see in the following sections how rationalizations like these, which today infest the minds of so many in the Christian world, are Stygian.

983. [2] There is no better way to see how marriage is heaven and adultery is hell than to consider their source. The source of true marriage love is the Lord's love for his church, which is why in the Word he is called *groom* or *husband* and the church is called *bride* or *wife*. This marriage defines the church in both a broad and narrow sense; in the narrow sense, the church is a person who has the church within them.

This demonstrates that the Lord's connection to a person in his church is the source of true love in marriage, but I should also explain how this works. The Lord's connection with a person in his church is a connection between goodness and truth. The goodness comes from the Lord, the truth is with the person, and the connection between them is called a *heavenly marriage*. This heavenly marriage sustains true marriage love between two partners who have this connection with the Lord. Above all, it demonstrates that true marriage love comes only from the Lord, and this love happens for those who experience the connection between the goodness and truth that come from the Lord. The Lord describes this as a reciprocal connection: "I am in my Father, and you in me, and I in you" (John 14:20).

[3] This connection, or marriage, has persisted since creation in the following fashion: man was created to understand what is true so that he can become truth, and woman was created to be inspired by what is good so that she can become goodness. When a man's understanding of truth is united with a woman's passion for goodness, there is a joining of the two minds into one.

This connection is spiritual marriage, from which marriage love descends. When two minds are joined together and make one mind, there is love between minds. This love, which is marriage love on a spiritual level, becomes a loving marriage on an earthly level as it descends into the body. Anyone who is so inclined can easily see that this is so: married partners who are inwardly attracted to each other in a mutual and complementary way are physically attracted to each other as well. We know that love descends into our body entirely from a mental impulse, as no love can develop without originating in the mind.

[4] Because the source of marriage love is the marriage between goodness and truth (heaven essentially *is* this

marriage between goodness and truth), it makes sense that the source of adultery is the marriage between evil and falsity (which is essentially hell).

Heaven is a marriage because everyone in heaven is involved in the marriage of goodness and truth. Hell is adultery because everyone in hell is involved in the marriage of evil and falsity. Marriage and adultery are therefore opposite to each other in the same way that heaven and hell are.

✄ ✄ ✄

984. [2] Humans are created to be love itself on both a spiritual and heavenly level and therefore to be the image and likeness of God. Spiritual love, or loving what is true, is in the image of God; and heavenly love, or loving what is good, is in the likeness of God. All the angels in the third heaven are in the likeness of God, and all the angels in the second heaven are in the image of God.

A person cannot become love in the image and likeness of God except by a marriage of goodness and truth. Goodness and truth love each other deeply and long to be united into one; and because divine love and divine truth come forth from the Lord unified, so must they be unified in an angel in heaven or a person in the church. This unification could never happen except in two minds married into one. As I said before, man is created to understand truth and become truth, and woman is created to yearn for and become goodness. They have this connection of goodness and truth, because marriage love—descending from this connection—is the actual means for a person to become love, that is, the image and likeness of God.

When two partners have a loving marriage that comes from the Lord, they love each other in a mutual and complementary way from the heart, that is, from deep within. Although they seem to be two people, they are one: two bodies but one life. This can be compared to the eyes, which are two as organs but one in vision; or the ears, which are two as organs but one in hearing. Even the arms and feet are two as limbs but one in function—the arms in performing tasks, the feet in walking—and the same is true with other parts of the body. This also relates to goodness and truth: an organ or limb on the right-hand side of the body relates to goodness, and one on the left-hand side relates to truth. It is the same for a husband and wife who have a genuinely loving marriage. They have two bodies but one life, and so in heaven married partners are referred to not as two angels but as one.

It is clear from this that through marriage a person becomes an embodiment of love and an embodiment of heaven: the image and likeness of the Lord.

[3] People are born wanting what is evil and false, and this desire is adulterous love. Adulterous love cannot be converted or transformed into spiritual love, which is the image of God, much less into heavenly love, which is the likeness of God, except by a marriage of goodness and truth that comes from the Lord. It cannot be completely transformed except by a marriage of two minds and two bodies.

Obviously, marriages are heavenly and adulteries are infernal. Marriage is the image of heaven, and genuine marriage love is the image of the Lord. Adultery is the image of hell, and adulterous love is the image of the devil. In the spiritual world, marriage love appears in the shape of an angel, and adulterous love appears in the shape of a devil. Store this away in your memory, dear reader, and ask yourself whether it is true. After you die, when you are living as a spiritual being, you will find out!

⚜ ⚜ ⚜

985. [2] From the holiness of marriage, we can deduce how foul and detestable adultery is. Everything in the human body, from head to toe, inside and out, corresponds to heaven. This is why a human being can be heaven in its least form and why angels and spirits, being forms of heaven, are in a perfect human form. All the reproductive organs of either sex, but especially the uterus, correspond to communities in the third or innermost heaven. This is because true marriage love is drawn from the love the Lord has for the church and from loving what is good and true, which is the kind of love the angels of the third heaven have. Marriage love descends from that heaven and belongs to it. It is innocence, which is the very essence of everything good in heaven. This is why a fetus in the womb is in a peaceful state, why a baby after it is born is in an innocent state, and why a mother is tenderhearted toward her child.

[3] The fact that the reproductive organs of each sex have this correspondence to heaven demonstrates that these organs are created to be holy and intended specifically for a loving marriage that is pure and faithful. They must not be defiled by an unfaithful and impure adulterous love, by which people convert the heaven inside them into hell. Adulterous love corresponds to the love of the deepest hell in the same way that marriage love corresponds to the love of the highest heaven, which is a love for the Lord that comes from him.

Marriage love is so holy and heavenly because it is initiated by the Lord himself deep within each person, and it descends into the outermost parts of the body in an orderly fashion until it fills the whole person with heavenly love. It imparts upon that individual the form of divine love, which is the form of heaven, and is the Lord's image, as I said before. Adulterous desire, on the other hand, starts in the outermost parts and with an impure and lascivious fire penetrates in a disorderly fashion to the person's innermost being. It always targets a person's sense of self-importance, which is nothing but wicked, and imparts upon it a hellish form, which is the image of the devil. It is because of this that a person who desires adultery and rejects marriage takes the shape of a devil.

[4] Since the reproductive organs of each sex correspond to communities in the third heaven, and the partners' desire corresponds to loving what is good and true, reproductive organs and the desire between partners likewise correspond to the Word. The Word is the divine truth united with divine goodness coming from the Lord. This is why the Lord is called the Word. Every detail in the Word is a marriage of goodness and truth, or a heavenly marriage.

This correspondence is a mystery as yet unknown on earth, but it has been demonstrated and proved to me by much experience. It explains how holy and heavenly are marriages and how filthy and devilish are adulteries. It also explains why adulterers regard divine truth as of no account and therefore too the Word. In fact, when speaking frankly, they blaspheme the holy things that are in the Word. They do this when they become spirits after they die, because all spirits are compelled to speak frankly so that their inner thoughts may be revealed.

⁂

986. [2] Everything enjoyable to us in this world is turned into the corresponding enjoyment in the spiritual world, and so this is true for the enjoyment of love in marriage and the enjoyment of adulterous desire. Marriage love is represented in the spiritual world by a young woman of such beauty that she arouses intense passion in the beholder. On the other hand, adulterous desire is represented by a hag so hideous that the beholder goes cold and all passion dies. In heaven, the angels' attractiveness depends on how strong their marriage love is; and in hell, the spirits' ugliness depends on the intensity of their desire for adultery. In other words, the faces, gestures, and voices of angels in heaven are full of life, depending on their marriage love; but to the degree that spirits in hell desire adultery, they have the look of death.

The same is true of their smell. In the spiritual world, the enjoyment of love in marriage is represented by the fragrance of various fruits and flowers, but the enjoyment of adultery is represented by the foul odor of dung or rotten things. The enjoyment of adultery actually turns into these things, because everything about adultery is spiritual filth, which is why the stench that wafts from the brothels in hell is enough to make you throw up.

988. [5] Marriages are intrinsically holy; that is, they have been holy since creation. We can see this from the fact that they are the wellspring of the human race; and since the angels in heaven come from the human race, marriages are also the wellspring of heaven. It is through marriages that not only the earth's surface is populated but also the heavens.

The whole purpose of creation is the human race and from the human race, heaven, where the divine being himself can dwell among his own as he actually is. By means of marriages, the procreation of the human race has been provided for according to divine order; and therefore it is obvious just how holy marriages are intrinsically, that is, from creation, and that they will remain so.

Earth could just as easily be populated by fornication and adultery as by marriage, but heaven could not. Hell stems from adultery, and heaven stems from marriage. Hell stems from adultery because adultery is the result of a marriage between evil and falsity, so hell in its entirety can be called an adultery. Heaven stems from marriage because marriages are the result of a marriage between goodness and truth, and so in its entirety heaven can be called a marriage (as we demonstrated above in this section).

In referring to hell as *adultery*, we mean it is a place where the desire for it (adulterous desire) predominates, whether in or out of wedlock. In calling heaven *marriage*, we mean it is a place where desiring it (marriage love) predominates.

[6] When the procreation of the human race occurs in marriages wherein prevails the holy love of goodness and truth given to us by the Lord, then it happens on earth as it is in heaven, and the Lord's kingdom on earth corresponds to his kingdom in heaven.

Heaven consists of communities arranged according to their various spiritual and heavenly proclivities. From this arrangement heaven gets its design, which is far more beautiful than any other design in the universe.

This same beautiful design could exist here on earth if children were born in marriages wherein prevails genuine marriage love. The many families descending from one ancestor would mirror the same number of heavenly societies with all their variety. Those families would be like various kinds of fruit trees: from each one would come an orchard with its unique kind of fruit, and all those orchards taken together would make up a celestial paradise. But I am speaking figuratively, with *trees* standing for those who are in the church, *orchards* standing for intelligence, *fruit* standing for leading a good life, and *paradise* standing for heaven.

I was told from heaven that this correspondence between families on earth and communities in heaven existed among the most ancient peoples, from whom was established the first church on this planet. This was also called the Golden Age by ancient writers, because it was a time governed by their love for the Lord, mutual love, innocence, peace, wisdom, and chastity in marriage. I was also told from heaven that in that day they had an inner revulsion to adultery, and they thought it was an abomination from hell.

⚜ ⚜ ⚜

989. [2] We said before that heaven comes from marriages and hell from adulteries. Now we should explain what this means. The hereditary evil that humans are born into does not come from Adam eating from the Tree of Knowledge; it comes from parents adulterating what is good and falsifying what is true, and this marriage of evil and falsity sustains the desire for adultery. The dominant love of parents is carried over and imprinted on their offspring by heredity and becomes their natural inclination. If the parents' dominant love is adultery, along with that comes wanting to do evil for the sake of falsity and wanting to lie for the sake of committing evil. This is the source of all our wickedness, and it is because of our wickedness that we choose hell.

It is apparent from this that we choose hell on account of adultery, unless we are reformed by the truth given to us by the Lord and by living according to that truth. Nor can anyone be reformed unless they avoid adultery as an infernal thing and love marriage as a heavenly thing. In no other way can we break or weaken the inheritance of evil in our offspring.

[3] We should realize that although we are born hellish on account of adulterous parents, still we are not destined for hell but for heaven. The Lord has made sure that none of us will be condemned to hell for inherited evil but only for the evil we actually do in our own life. This is evident from the fact that those who die as infants are adopted by the Lord, educated under his guidance in heaven, and saved.

All of this proves that even though each of us is a hell on account of inborn evil, we are not born destined for hell but for heaven. The same is true of everyone born as a result of adultery, if they themselves do not commit adultery. Being an adulterer means living in a marriage between wickedness and falsehood, thinking evil and false things because you enjoy thinking about them, and doing them because you love doing them. Everyone who does this becomes an adulterer. It is a matter of divine justice that none of us pays the penalty for our parents' wickedness but only for our own. The Lord makes sure that inherited evil does not come back after we die. Our own evil does come back, and it is for this that a person is punished after death.

⚜ ⚜ ⚜

990. [2] We said previously that the difference between marriage love and adulterous desire is like the difference between heaven and hell. The same is true for the difference between the pleasures of those two desires, since pleasures come entirely from the loves that are their source. The pleasures of adulterous desire come entirely from pursuing evil purposes and ultimately from wrongdoing. The pleasures of marriage love come entirely from the joy of pursuing good ends and ultimately from doing good.

To the extent people enjoy the evil they are engaged in, they enjoy adulterous desire, because the desire to commit adultery comes from enjoying doing evil. Hardly anyone can believe that this is where the pleasure of adultery comes from, but nonetheless that is its origin. And so it is obvious that the pleasure of adultery rises up from the deepest hell. On the other hand, the pleasure of marriage love is celestial pleasure, because it comes from wanting to connect goodness with truth and from wanting to do good things. This pleasure descends from the innermost, or third, heaven, which is governed by a love for the Lord given to us by him.

[3] And so we can assert that the distinction between those two kinds of pleasure is like the distinction between heaven

and hell. But amazingly people believe that the pleasures of marriage and of adultery are similar. Nevertheless, there is this difference between them, as we have just described. In fact, no one can clearly grasp the difference, except for those who enjoy marriage love. People who enjoy marriage love have a keen sense that there is nothing impure, unchaste, or lascivious in enjoying it and that enjoying adulterous desire is nothing but impure, unchaste, and lascivious. They sense that whatever is unchaste rises up from below and that whatever is chaste descends from above. Those who enjoy adultery do not realize this because anything hellish seems heavenly to them.

This proves that marriage love, even in its physical expression, is purity and chastity itself and that adulterous desire in all its expression is outright impurity and unchastity. Since the pleasure of each desire looks similar on the outside (although they are totally different on the inside, being opposites), the Lord makes sure that the pleasures of adultery cannot rise up into heaven and that the pleasures of marriage cannot sink down into hell. Still, there is some correspondence between heaven and procreation that results from adultery, though no correspondence between heaven and the actual pleasures of adultery.

991. [2] I have said that love in marriage, which is an earthly thing, derives from loving what is good and true, which is a spiritual thing. This spiritual element is within the earthly desire for marriage, as a cause is in its effect. From this marriage between what is good and what is true comes a desire to be productive, that is, to use truth to do good and to generate truth from good impulses. It is from this desire to be productive that married partners get their desire to procreate, which is the source of all their pleasure and delight.

Likewise, adulterous desire, which is an earthly thing, comes from wanting what is evil and false, which is a spiritual thing. This spiritual element is within the earthly desire to commit adultery, as a cause is in its effect. From this marriage between what is evil and what is false, [expressed] by means of their desire, also comes a desire to be productive—that is, to do evil by means of lies and to generate lies from wicked impulses. It is from this desire that they get a desire to procreate in adulterous relationships, and this is the source of all their pleasure and delight.

[3] The intimacy involved in reproduction is so thoroughly enjoyable and pleasurable because undertaking and accomplishing some useful purpose has brought with it since creation every sort of enjoyment, satisfaction, bliss, and happiness in all of heaven and all the world. The enjoyment reaches greater and greater heights to eternity, as the usefulness of the endeavor increases in value and worthiness. This explains why the pleasure of reproduction is so great, greater than all other pleasures: it is greater because its function—the procreation of the human race and ultimately heaven—is more useful than other functions.

[4] This is also the source of the pleasure and enjoyment in adultery. However, because breeding in adultery corresponds to doing evil by means of lies and generating lies from evil impulses, the pleasure and enjoyment gradually grows weaker, is cheapened, and ultimately becomes disgustingly nauseating.

As we said before, the pleasure of marriage love is heavenly pleasure, and pleasure in adultery is infernal pleasure. The pleasure of adultery, then, comes from a kind of polluted fire which, while it lasts, simulates the pleasure of a healthy love but essentially is a pleasure that comes from hating what is good and true. Because this is its origin, there is no love between two adulterers, except for the kind of desire that comes from hatred. The result is that they are connected outwardly but not inwardly; outwardly they are on fire, but inwardly they are frozen. After a short while, the fire goes out and is replaced by frigidity, either from impotence or from the kind of disgust one has for filth.

[5] I was allowed to observe the fundamental nature of adulterous desire. On the inside it was like murderous hatred, and on the outside it seemed like the flames that come from burning filthy, rotten, putrid dung. And as this fire and its enjoyment burnt itself out, the [couple's] conversation and time together was gradually drained of life and the hatred started to show—first as a kind of contempt, then avoidance, then rejection, and ultimately cursing and fighting. It is amazing that although they hated each other, they were able to have sex with each other and even feel their hateful pleasure as a loving pleasure, when it was no more than the pleasure of scratching an itch.

[6] I cannot describe nor would you believe how the spirits in hell take pleasure in hating and ultimately hurting people. Hurting people is their heart's delight; they call it heaven. The pleasure they take in hurting people is drawn entirely from the hatred and spite they have for things that are good and true. On this account, they get furiously whipped up in a murderous and devilish hatred against heaven—particularly against those who come from heaven and worship the Lord. They yearn desperately to torture them; and because they are unable to torture their bodies, they try to torture their souls.

It is, therefore, this hateful pleasure, converted ultimately into fire and injected into their lustful flesh, which at that instant becomes the pleasure of adultery; the soul, where that hatred lurks, temporarily withdraws. This is why I call hell adultery and why adulterers are so totally merciless, savage, and cruel; this is now a hellish marriage.

[7] Adultery burns on the outside, but on the inside it is cold. What is on the inside does not produce what is on the outside, as happens in marriage, but rather they battle against each other. When the woman wants to have sex, the man feels impotent, and all the more so if she is insistent. At that point, his inner coldness reaches his sexual appetite, seeps into his outer fire, and extinguishes it, rejecting that fire as useless. It gets to the point that even his craving for rape, which likewise fuels this filthy fire, dies out.

⚜ ⚜ ⚜

992. [2] As we said, the desire to commit adultery is like a fire that comes from burning filth. It burns out quickly, turns into coldness, and then turns into a rejection that amounts to hatred. Marriage love is the opposite: it is a fire fueled by wanting what is good and true and by the pleasure of doing good things. In other words, it is fueled by love for the Lord and toward other people. This fire is celestial in its origin, and it is every bit as full of pleasure as are the countless pleasures and blessings of heaven.

I have been told that marriage love involves recurring delights and comforts that are so many and so great that they cannot be expressed in numbers or descriptions. They multiply and get better to eternity. These pleasures arise from married partners wanting to be of a single mind, with heaven and its marriage of goodness and truth from the Lord collaborating in the union.

[3] I would like to relate some things about the marriages of angels in heaven. They say that their sexual potency is unlimited. After sex, they are never tired, let alone sad, but vigorous and cheerful. They spend the night in each other's embrace as though they were born to be a single person. Their climaxes are long-lasting; and when they try they never fail, because

lovemaking without climax is like a clogged water pipe—the climax opens up the pipe so it can keep flowing. This creates a connection so that they may be one flesh. The man's vital force combines itself with the woman's vital force and they bond together. They say that the pleasure of their climax cannot be expressed in the words of any language in this world and cannot even be imagined in anything other than spiritual ideas; even these do not suffice. The angels told me this.

⚜ ⚜ ⚜

993. [2] In true marriage love, there are pleasures beyond what numbers or words can express. This makes sense because marriage is the foundation of all heavenly and spiritual love, being the means by which we become love. Because of their marriage, one partner loves the other like goodness loves truth (or truth loves goodness), which is a representation of how the Lord loves heaven and his church.

Love like this cannot exist except in a marriage in which the husband is truth and the wife is goodness. When we have become love through this kind of marriage, we also love the Lord and love other people, and we consequently love everything that is good and everything that is true. Nothing can come from a person who is love, except for love of every kind. This is why marriage love is the foundation of all the love in heaven; and because it is, it is also the foundation of all the pleasure and joy in heaven. Love is the source of all pleasure and joy.

[3] We can conclude from this that marriage love is the origin and cause of heavenly joy of every type and every level of intensity, and from the happiness of marriage we can deduce the unhappiness of adultery. The desire to commit adultery is the foundation of all infernal love, which is not really love but hatred. From adulterous desire springs every kind of

hatred, against God, against other people, and against all the good and true things in heaven and the church in general. This is why adulterous love is so thoroughly unhappy. The result of adultery is that a person becomes a form of hell; and the result of wanting to commit adultery is that a person becomes an image of the devil, as I said before.

In the book *Heaven and Hell* (§386), you can read how, in a marriage that is a truly loving one, the pleasure and happiness grows enormously until it equals the pleasure and happiness of even the innermost heaven. You can also read how the unpleasantness and unhappiness in a marriage where adulterous desire prevails grows in cruelty until it reaches even the deepest hell.

⚔ ⚔ ⚔

995. [2] True love in marriage comes only from the Lord. The reason it comes only from the Lord is because it descends from the love the Lord has for heaven and the church and therefore from wanting what is good and true. The Lord is where goodness comes from, and heaven and his church are where truth is. It is logical, then, that true marriage love is first and foremost loving the Lord. This is why no one can enjoy true love in marriage—with its comforts, pleasures, blessings, and joys—except for a person who acknowledges the Lord alone, that is, acknowledges that the Trinity is in him. Those who approach the Father as a separate person or approach the Holy Spirit as a separate person, and do not approach them as being within the Lord, do not enjoy marriage love.

Genuine marriage love exists in the third heaven in particular because the angels there love the Lord, acknowledge him alone as God, and do what he commands. For them, loving him means doing what he commands, and his commandments are the truth in which they receive him. The Lord joins with them and they with him: they are within the Lord because they do what is good, and the Lord is within them because he is within the truth. This is heavenly marriage, and it is from this that true love in marriage descends.

996. [2] Because true marriage love is first and foremost a love for the Lord given to us by him, it is also innocence. Innocence is loving the Lord as our father by doing what he commands and wanting to be led by him, like a small child, and not by ourselves. Because innocence is loving the Lord, it is the soul of every good thing. We have heaven in ourselves, or we are in heaven, to the degree we love marriage, because to that degree we are innocent.

True love in marriage is innocence, and so the playfulness of married couples is like young children playing together. The intensity of their love for each other determines how playful they are with each other. We see this during every couple's honeymoon stage, when their love mimics a truly loving marriage. The innocence of love in marriage is referred to in the Word by the *nakedness* which did not embarrass Adam and his wife. There is nothing lascivious or shameful between the partners, any more than there is between young children who are naked together.

997. [4] Since the fundamental essence of marriage love is a love for the Lord given to us by him, and therefore innocence, it is also true that marriage love is peace as it exists in heaven among the angels. If innocence is the essence of everything good, peace is the essence of every pleasure that comes from what is good and is therefore the essence of the partners' enjoyment of each other. All joy comes from love, and marriage love is the foundation of all love in heaven, and so peace itself dwells especially in marriage love.

You can read in *Revelation Explained* 365 about how peace is a contentment of heart and soul that happens when the Lord connects with heaven and the church. Goodness joins with truth, putting an end to their contentious battle with evil and falsity. Marriage love descends from these unions, and so all the delights of this love descend from, and draw their essence from, heavenly peace. This peace shines as a heavenly blessing from the faces of married partners who enjoy this love and see each other in its light. A heavenly blessing like this, stirring the pleasure of their love deep inside, can also be called peace and can exist only in those who are able to be connected so deeply that their very hearts are joined.

✧ ✧ ✧

998. [4] The measure and quality of our intelligence and wisdom depend on the intensity of marriage love. Marriage love comes from wanting what is good and true, the way the effect comes from its cause or something earthly comes from its spiritual origin.

The angels of the three heavens likewise get their intelligence and wisdom entirely from the marriage between what is good and what is true. Intelligence and wisdom are nothing other than receiving light and heat from the Lord as our sun, which means receiving divine truth combined with divine goodness and receiving divine goodness combined with divine truth. This is the marriage between goodness and truth that comes from the Lord.

That this is so becomes quite obvious from the reactions of the angels in heaven. When they are separated from their spouses, they are still intelligent but are not wise; however, when they are in the company of their spouses, they are wise as well as intelligent. It amazed me how they come into a wise state of mind by turning toward their partners. In the spiritual world, a connection between what is good and what is true happens by means of a gaze, the wife being what is good and the husband being what is true; and as the truth turns toward what is good, the truth comes alive.

By intelligence and wisdom I do not mean making brilliant arguments about what is true and good but rather having the ability to discern what is true and good and to understand it. We get our ability to do this from the Lord.

999. [2] Genuine marriage love gives us the power to be protected from hell by giving us the power to be protected from the evil and falsity rising up from hell. Marriage love connects us with the Lord, and it is the Lord alone who prevails over all of hell. In fact, it is by means of marriage love that we are open to heaven and the church. The Lord constantly protects heaven and the church from the evil and falsity that surge up from hell; and in this way he likewise protects all people who truly love marriage, since you will find heaven and the church among these and no others.

Heaven and the church are a marriage between what is good and what is true, which, as I said previously, is where marriage love comes from. This is why people can find peace in marriage love, which is a deep joy in their heart coming from being totally safe from hell and protected against the infestations of evil and falsity that come from hell.

1000. [4] When people who truly love marriage become angels after they die, they revert to their youth. Even if they had been worn out by old age, husbands become young men and their wives young women. Both partners enjoy the prime of youth, when their marriage love first enriched their life with new pleasures and kindled their lovemaking with the thought of having children.

Those who had resisted adultery as sinful and were initiated into a loving marriage by the Lord when they were in the world achieve this state superficially at first and then more and more deeply for all eternity. Because they are always growing more youthful within, a genuinely loving marriage gets stronger and stronger and partakes in its wholesome pleasures. These pleasures, which have been reserved for marriage since the creation of the world, are the wholesome pleasures of the innermost heavens. They spring from the love the Lord has for heaven and the church and the subsequent desire goodness and truth have for each other, which is the source of all joy in heaven.

In heaven, the partners become youthful in this way because they are commencing a marriage between goodness and truth. Within goodness there is a constant urge to love what is true, and within truth is a constant urge to love what is good. In a marriage like this, the wife is the embodiment of goodness and the husband is the embodiment of truth. It is this urge that causes them to completely cast off their stern, sad, and shriveled old age and embrace a lively, cheerful, and blooming youth. Then the urge comes alive and turns into joy.

[5] I was told from heaven that these married partners lead a life full of love, which can only be described as a life of total joy. I was also told that people who enjoy true love in marriage while they live in this world come into a heavenly marriage after they die—a marriage between goodness and truth that originates in the Lord's marriage to the church.

It is quite obvious from this that although married partners in heaven have relationships as they do on earth, children are not born from their marriages. As I said before, instead of having children, they have goodness and truth and the wisdom that results. This is why the spiritual meaning of *having a baby, childbirth,* and *reproduction* in the Word is spiritual babies, spiritual childbirth, and spiritual reproduction. *Sons* and *daughters* mean the goodness and truth in the church; *daughter-in-law, mother-in-law,* and *father-in-law* have related meanings.

One can clearly see that marriages on earth correspond to marriages in heaven and that people come into this correspondence after they die. That is to say, they go from an earthly, physical marriage into a spiritual, heavenly marriage, which is what heaven and heavenly joy actually are.

1001. The angels' beauty comes entirely from loving marriage, each angel according to how intense their love is. All angels are expressions of their feelings. They are not allowed to misrepresent their feelings on their face, and so their expression is a direct reflection of their mind. As long as they love marriage, they also love the Lord, love other people, love goodness and truth, and love wisdom. All this love gives expression to their face and lights up their eyes with life. Add peace and innocence to this, and their beauty is complete, comparable to the beautiful expressions of the angels of the inmost heaven. These are truly human expressions.

1002. [2] From everything presented so far, we can infer the good that comes from being chaste in marriage and the beneficial effects of chastity when a person avoids adultery as a sin against God. Chastity has beneficial effects on the married partners themselves, on their children and descendants, and on communities in heaven. The beneficial effects of chastity specifically on the married partners themselves are spiritual and heavenly love, intelligence and wisdom, innocence and peace, the power to be kept safe from hell and from the evil and falsity that come from hell, and also countless joys and eternal happiness. To say that those who live in a chaste marriage enjoy all of these things is consistent with what I have previously stated.

The specific beneficial effect of chastity on children and descendants is that families do not inherit so many different kinds of evil, or evils of such magnitude, given that the dominant love of parents is passed on to their children and their descendants (even many generations distant) and becomes part of their heredity. These character traits are broken or diminished by parents who avoid adultery as something hellish and desire marriage as something heavenly.

[3] The beneficial effects of chastity that are specific to communities in heaven are that chaste marriages are the delight of heaven, its breeding ground, and its foundation. Chaste marriages impart delight to heaven, because there is a communication between the two. By reproduction, they are heaven's breeding ground. And they are its foundation through their power over hell, since devilish spirits become enraged in the presence of marriage love, go mad, lose control, and cast themselves into the depths.

1003. [3] By listing and describing the beneficial effects of chaste marriages, we can deduce the harmful effects of adultery, because the harmful results are the opposite of the beneficial results.

- Instead of loving spiritual and heavenly things like people in chaste marriages do, those engaging in adultery love infernal and devilish things.

- Instead of being intelligent and wise like those living chastely in marriages are, those engaging in adultery are insane and stupid.

- Instead of being innocent and at peace like those living in chaste marriages are, those engaging in adultery are deceitful and find no peace.

- Instead of having the power to stay safe from hell like those living chastely in marriage do, those engaging in adultery are themselves Asmodean demons and hells.

- Instead of being beautiful like those living in a chaste marriage are, those living in adultery are disfigured, their character determining what sort of monster they are.

Ultimately, this is their fate: the total impotence to which they have reduced themselves renders their life totally devoid of energy and inspiration. They pass the time alone in the wilderness, the embodiment of lethargy and weariness with life.

1004. [2] True love can only exist between two people, just as the Lord's love for heaven or the love he has for the church can only exist between the two parties. Heaven is unified by the Lord and within him. Everyone in heaven must be united in mutual love by loving the Lord. The angel in heaven who does not become united with the others in mutual love does not belong in heaven. Likewise, the church is unified by the Lord and within him, and any person in the church who does not become united with others in mutual love does not belong in the church.

Going a step further, everything in the whole of heaven and the entire world is related to two things we call goodness and truth, and everything in heaven and on earth exists and is sustained by the combination of these two into one. Because they are united, goodness is within truth and truth within goodness, and truth is defined by goodness and goodness by truth. Each recognizes the other as its reciprocating counterpart, acting and reacting in turn.

A loving marriage between a husband and wife comes from this universal marriage of goodness and truth. The husband was created to understand what is true and the wife was created to want what is good, so that truth and goodness can take shape together—a human shape in the image of God.

Because goodness is created to be defined by truth, truth is created to be defined by goodness, and they interact reciprocally, it is not possible to have one true thing united with two separate good things and vice versa. Nor can there be one intellect united with two different wills and vice versa; and neither can there be one person spiritually united with two different churches. In the same way, one man cannot be deeply united with two women. A deep union is like the union of the soul and the heart: the wife's soul is her husband, and the husband's heart is his wife. The husband communicates and joins his soul with his wife in lovemaking: his soul is in his seed, the wife receives it with all her heart, and from this the two become one.

[3] Each and every thing in the body of one partner focuses on its counterpart in the body of the other. This is a real marriage, possible only between two people. From creation, everything in the mind and body of a man has its counterpart in the mind and body of his wife so that every single part of each focuses on its counterpart and seeks to be united with it. It is this focus and urge that constitute marriage love.

All the parts of the body, which we call members, viscera, and organs, are nothing other than earthly, physical forms corresponding to spiritual forms in the mind. Each and every part of the body corresponds to some part of the mind. Whatever the mind wants or thinks, the body instantly acts on the suggestion. In the same way, when two minds act as one, the two bodies are inclined to be united so that they are no longer two but are one flesh. Marriage love is wanting to become one flesh, and the love is as strong as that wish.

[4] I am permitted to confirm this with an amazing fact from heaven: there are married partners in heaven whose love is so strong that they are able to be one flesh. They can be so whenever they want, and at that moment they look like a single person. I saw this happen, and I spoke with the couple. They said:

> We have one life; we are like goodness living within truth and truth living within goodness. We are like the pairings within one human being, for example, like the two halves of the brain enclosed within the meninges, the two chambers of the heart within a common membrane, or the two lobes of the lungs similarly enclosed. Although there are two of each, they are one in life and in their life's work, which is the function they perform.
>
> Because of this, we lead a life of fulfillment together in heaven. It is what living in heaven with its infinite blessings is all about, because heaven actually comes from the Lord's marriage to it. All the angels of heaven are within the Lord, and the Lord is within them.

[5] They spoke further:

> It is impossible for us to even consider pursuing a different wife or another woman, because that would be turning heaven into hell. An angel merely thinking about doing so falls from heaven.

In closing, they said:

> Spirits who are on an earthly plane cannot believe it is possible for us to have this kind of relationship. As far as merely earthly people are concerned, marriage does not come from a spiritual origin—the marriage between goodness and

truth—but from an earthly origin. For them, there is no union of minds but only a bodily union driven by a carnal wantonness, which comes from a universal principle implanted and inborn by design in everything animate or inanimate: anything with a life force wants to reproduce its own likeness, and it wants to increase its own kind infinitely and eternally. The offspring of Jacob, who were the sons of Israel, being but earthly men, had marriages of the flesh and not of the spirit; so a concession was made to them to take multiple wives, because they were so stubborn.

⚜ ⚜ ⚜

1005. [2] By imagining different men's seed mixed together in the uterus of one woman, anyone can appreciate that adultery is hell and an abomination. The inmost component of human life is latent within the seed. It is the starting point of new life, which is what makes it holy. Rendering this a commodity alongside the inmost and original parts of other men—which is what happens in adultery—is profane.

This is why adultery is hell, and hell is frequently called adultery. Adultery is an abomination, because nothing but rottenness can ensue from such a mixture—even though it comes from a spiritual origin.

[3] This is why foul odors of every kind are found in the brothels of hell; and when heaven's light is shined into them, the adulterers—female and male alike—can be seen lying together like pigs in their own filth. Amazingly enough, they are as happy to be lying in filth as are pigs. However, these brothels are kept shut, because whenever they are opened up, the reek that escapes would make you throw up.

It is entirely different in chaste marriages, in which the man's life force adds itself to his wife's by way of his seed. This creates an intimate connection, causing them to be not two but one flesh. As they connect by means of this seed, the love in their marriage grows, and along with it comes every blessing of heaven.

⚜ ⚜ ⚜

1006. [2] You should know that adultery can be more or less infernal or abominable. Since adultery corresponds to the adulterating of goodness and to the falsifying of truth that results, adultery that arises from more grievous evil and falsity is more serious, and adultery that arises from milder evil and falsity is less serious. Adulterating goodness is what evil actually is, and perverting the truth is what falsity actually is.

The hells have been arranged in correspondence to these adulterations and falsifications, both in their general design and in each of their parts: cadaverous hells for those who took delight in forcing themselves on their wives, fecal hells for those who took delight in seducing young women, horribly slimy hells for those who took delight in all sorts of perverse and promiscuous sexual activity, and filthy hells for the rest. There are sodomitical hells for those who engage in evil because they want to dominate others only to enjoy dominating other people and not for any useful purpose.

[3] Adultery like that of a son with his mother or aunt emanates from those who separate faith from good works, both in doctrine and in their actions; adultery like that of a father with his daughter-in-law emanates from those who study the Word only for the sake of their reputation and not for any spiritual purpose; adultery like that of a brother with his sister emanates from those who believe that sins are forgiven by the Holy Supper and not by changing how they live; unspeakable acts with animals emanate from those who totally deny the Lord's divinity; and so forth. Spirits are in hells like

these because hells correspond to the adulterating and polluting of goodness and truth.

⚜ ⚜ ⚜

1007. To sum up, every time evil and falsity are joined in the spiritual world, an aura of adultery is emitted. This only happens when it is done by those who have the wrong ideas about religion *and* lead evil lives, not when it is done by those who have the wrong ideas about religion but lead good lives. The latter do not compound evil with falsity; the former do.

Adultery especially emanates from preachers who have taught false ideas and led evil lives, since they have also adulterated and falsified the Word. They stir up adultery even if they did not commit adultery in the world. This is an adultery called *priestly adultery* and is distinct from other kinds of adultery. It demonstrates that the source of adultery is the loving and subsequent combining of evil and falsity.

⚜ ⚜ ⚜

1008. [2] Adultery is less abhorrent to Christians than it is to other peoples, including some uncivilized peoples, because in the Christian world today there is a marriage of evil and falsity rather than a marriage of goodness and truth. A religion that teaches faith to be separate from good works is a religion that teaches truth to be separate from goodness. Truth apart from goodness is not truth (in fact, when examined from an inner perspective, it is falsity), and goodness apart from truth is not goodness (when examined from an inner perspective, it is evil). This is why in the Christian religion there are evil and false ideas, which are the source of the desire for and approval of the adultery that flows in from hell. This is why in the Christian world adultery is thought permissible and is practiced without shame.

As I said before, the joining of evil and falsity is spiritual adultery, which is the source of earthly adultery by correspondence. This is why *adultery* and *fornication* in the Word stand for the adulteration of goodness and the falsification of truth. Therefore, Babylon is called *the whore* in the book of Revelation, and Jerusalem is likewise called in the Old Testament. It is why the Lord called the Jewish people an *adulterous race* who were *from their father, the Devil*. (For more on this from the Word, see *Revelation Explained* 141.)

※ ※ ※

1009. [2] If you resist adultery for some reason other than because it is a sin and against God, you are still an adulterer. For example, people can resist adultery because they are afraid of the civil law and its penalties; are afraid of losing their reputation and the respect that goes with it; are afraid of sexually transmitted diseases; are afraid of getting into fights with their wife, causing stress at home; are afraid of being beaten by the servants of an angry husband; or because they do not have enough money or are too stingy; or are incapable as the result of self-abuse, old age, impotence, or sickness. In fact, if they refrain due to some instinct or moral code but not also due to divine law, they are still inwardly unchaste and adulterers. They still believe that adultery is not a sin, and so in their spirit they maintain that adultery is allowable and they commit adultery spiritually but not with their body. When they become spirits after they die, they speak out openly in favor of adultery and indulge in it without shame.

In the spiritual world, I was given a chance to observe some young women who considered promiscuous behavior wrong because it was contrary to divine law, and I saw some young women who did not think so but refrained from it to avoid a bad reputation that might frighten off suitors. I saw this last group wrapped in a dark cloud, sinking down toward those below. I saw the first group wrapped in a bright white cloud, rising up toward those above.

1010. [4] Now that I have said all this about adultery, let me define what it is. Adultery is any promiscuous behavior that ruins marriage love. It is promiscuous behavior of a husband with another man's wife or with a woman who is either a widow, a virgin, or a prostitute—when it occurs as the result of a disgust with or rejection of his marriage. Likewise, it is promiscuous behavior of a wife with another man, married or not, when it occurs for the same reason. Adultery is also the promiscuous behavior of any unmarried man with another man's wife or of any unmarried woman with another woman's husband, because it destroys love in marriage by turning the minds of those people away from their marriage and toward adultery.

Taking pleasure in different partners—even if they are prostitutes—is a pleasure of adultery, because this pleasure ruins the pleasures of marriage. The pleasure in taking a woman's virginity without intending marriage is also a pleasure of adultery; in that case, a man's only interest in marriage becomes the taking of a woman's virginity; and once this has been accomplished, he loathes the marriage. In a word, any promiscuous act that destroys the idea of marriage and extinguishes marriage love is adultery or related to adultery. On the other hand, promiscuity that does not destroy marriage or extinguish marriage love is fornication, overwhelming a person with a physical urge to marry when—for various reasons—marriage cannot yet be entered into.

The Seventh Commandment
You Shall Not Kill

1012. [3] All the precepts of the Ten Commandments, as

is the case with everything in the Word, contain two inner meanings in addition to the highest meaning, which is a third inner meaning. The first, which is not far from the literal meaning, is called the spiritual-moral meaning. The second, which is further from the literal meaning, is called the heavenly-spiritual meaning.

The more nearly literal, or spiritual-moral, meaning of *you shall not kill* is that you should not hate your peers or anyone else and that you should not undermine them with insults and humiliation. When you do this, you damage or kill the reputation and respect they need in order to live among their own peers in public life. As a result, they are dead to their community, because they are considered among the vile and deplorable with whom one does not associate.

When this happens as the result of animosity, hatred, or revenge, it is murder, and many people even in this world treat it as seriously as physical murder. People who engage in this are deemed as guilty in the eyes of the angels as if they had physically killed someone. Animosity, hatred, and revenge breathe murder and long for it but are held back or reined in by fear of the law, of retaliation, or of the loss of reputation. Nevertheless, those three attitudes—animosity, hatred, and revenge—are an impulse toward murder, and every impulse is like an action: the impulse transforms into action as soon as the fear is removed. This is what the Lord teaches us in Matthew:

> You have heard that it was said to those of ancient times, "You shall not murder"; and "whoever murders shall be liable to judgment." But I say to you that if you are angry with a brother or sister, you will be liable to judgment; and if you insult a brother or sister, you will be liable to the council; and if you say "You fool," you will be liable to the hell of fire. (Matthew 5:21–22)

[4] The heavenly-spiritual meaning of the teaching *you shall not kill*, which is more removed from the literal meaning, is that you should not take away from people their belief in God and their love for him. In doing this, you take away their spiritual life; and this is true murder, because spiritual life makes a person human. Their bodily life merely supports their spiritual life the way a short-term objective supports the ultimate goal.

Murder on a moral level is channeled from this spiritual murder, so that when you engage in the one you are also engaging in the other. If you want to take someone's spiritual life away from them but are unable to do so, you hate that individual, because you hate what the person believes and loves and therefore you hate the actual person. These three— the spiritual murder of what someone believes and loves, the moral murder of someone's reputation and respect, and the physical murder of a person's body—progress in that order, one after the other, in a cause-and-effect relationship.

1013. [2] Hell is actual murder, that is, where actual murder comes from. Everyone in hell hates the Lord and hates heaven, because they hate anything good and anything true. This is actual murder, since the goodness and truth we get from the Lord is what makes us human. Destroying that goodness and truth is actually destroying our humanity, that is, killing us.

[3] People in this world do not yet know that this is what spirits in hell are like. Those who allow themselves to be influenced by hell and who are therefore going to hell after they die do not seem to us like they hate being good and being truthful or like they hate heaven, much less hate the Lord. While living in this world, everyone has an outer being, which is taught and trained from infancy to pretend to be honorable

and decent, to be just and fair, and to be good and to be truthful. Yet to the degree they lead a wicked life, hatred lies hidden in their spirit; and because this hatred is in their spirit, it bursts out whenever that outer being is discarded, as is the case after death.

[4] Their infernal hatred toward everyone who embraces good is deadly, because it is a hatred of the Lord. This becomes particularly obvious when we consider how much they enjoy being wicked—so much so that it exceeds every other enjoyment they have. It is a fire that feeds on their desire to destroy souls.

I also learned that their pleasure does not come from hating the people they are trying to destroy; it comes from hating the Lord himself. It is the Lord who makes us human, and the humanity we get from the Lord is being good and being truthful. It makes sense that actual murder comes from hell, because those in hell—driven by their hatred for the Lord—desire to kill that humanity, which is being good and being truthful.

⚜ ⚜ ⚜

1014. [2] From what I have said so far, it is obvious that all who embrace evil in their life, and therefore falsity, are murderers. They are enemies and haters of what is good and what is true, since evil hates goodness and falsity hates the truth. Bad people do not even know they have this kind of hatred until they become spirits, but then hatred becomes the absolute joy of their life.

This is why a delight in wrongdoing—fueled by hatred—emanates perpetually from hell, where everyone is bad. On the other hand, a delight in doing good things—fueled by love—emanates perpetually from heaven, where everyone is good. And so we have these two opposite auras facing off against each other midway between heaven and hell, fighting each other. We are in this middle area when we are in this world. If we engage in evil and justify it with falsehood, we cross over into hellish territory and come to enjoy our malicious evildoing; if we embrace good and strengthen it with the truth, we cross over into heavenly territory and come to enjoy helping others because we love it.

[3] The enjoyment of malicious wrongdoing that emanates from hell is the enjoyment of killing; but because such people cannot kill the body, they try to kill the spirit. Killing the spirit is taking away the spiritual life that is the life of heaven. It is clear from this that the teaching *you shall not kill* includes not hating other people, as well as not hating the goodness in the church and the truth it teaches. If you hate being good and being truthful, you hate other people, and hating is wanting to kill. This is why the Lord calls the Devil (meaning hell, collectively) *a murderer from the beginning* (John 8:44).

⚜ ⚜ ⚜

1015. [2] Hatred, which is wanting to commit murder, is the opposite of loving the Lord and the opposite of loving other people. If these two kinds of love create heaven in us, then obviously hatred, because it is the opposite, creates hell in us. Hellfire is nothing other than hatred, and so hell seems to burn with a hideous red glow according to the type of hatred and its intensity, and it seems to burn with hideous flames according to the type of vengeance that flares up from that hatred and its intensity.

Because hatred and love are diametrically opposed, and hatred creates hell in us in the same way love creates heaven, the Lord teaches us,

> So when you are offering your gift at the altar, if you remember that your brother or sister has something against you,

leave your gift there before the altar and go; first be reconciled to your brother or sister, and then come and offer your gift. Come to terms quickly with your accuser while you are on the way to court with him, or your accuser may hand you over to the judge, and the judge to the guard, and you will be thrown into prison. Truly I tell you, you will never get out until you have paid the last penny. (Matthew 5:23–26)

Being handed over to the judge, by the judge to the guard, and being thrown into prison by him describes the situation of people who embrace hatred after death because they had been hateful to those with whom they associated in this world. *Prison* means hell, and *paying the last penny* means the punishment, referred to as eternal fire.

1016. [2] Hatred is hellfire, and obviously it must be removed before love, which is heavenly fire, can flow in with its light and give us new life. In no way can that hellfire be removed until we know where the hatred comes from and what it is, and then we turn away and flee from it.

By heredity, everyone hates other people. We are all born loving ourselves and worldly ambition, and we are seized with burning hatred toward those who do not agree with us or do not give us preferential treatment—especially those who get in the way of what we want. It is not possible for us to love ourselves above all things and at the same time love the Lord, and it is not possible to pursue worldly ambition above all things and at the same time love other people. No one can serve two masters at the same time without hating and condemning one and honoring and loving the other. Those who want to control everybody else especially have this hatred, while the rest have a mere animosity toward others.

[3] Now let us define hatred: hatred harbors within itself a fire that is the urge to kill people, and that fire shows up as anger. Good people can seem to hate evil and be angry. It is not hatred, though, but an aversion to evil; and it is not anger but a zeal for good, in which is hidden a heavenly fire. Although it is the evil they are opposed to, they act angry with the other person in order to remove that evil. In this way, they are considering what is in that person's best interest.

✣　✣　✣

1017. When we refrain from hatred, reject it, and avoid it as something diabolical, then love, kindness, mercy, and forgiveness flow into us from the Lord through heaven. Now for the first time our endeavors are undertaken with goodwill. Previously, however good our endeavors might have looked from the outside, they were done from self-love and worldly desire. When we were not rewarded for our deeds, hatred lurked within them.

To the degree this hatred is not removed, we remain on a purely earthly plane, and a person who is only on the earthly plane is influenced by every sort of inherited evil. We cannot become spiritual until hatred is torn out by its very root, which is the desire to control other people. The fire of heaven, which is spiritual love, cannot influence someone as long as the fire of hell, which is hatred, is in its way and blocking it.

✣　✣　✣

The Eighth Commandment
You Shall Not Bear False Witness

1019. [2] In the narrowest sense, *bearing false witness* means lying about other people by falsely accusing them. In a deeper sense, it means claiming that something just is unjust or that something unjust is just and confirming it with lies. The deepest meaning of *bearing false witness* is to distort the true and good things in the Word or, on the other hand, to corroborate false teachings by convincing people with bad logic, misrepresentations, making things up, misusing facts, creating convoluted arguments, and the like. Such arguments and our efforts to convince others of them are *false testimony*, because we are presenting false evidence.

Obviously, not only does *bearing false witness* mean giving false testimony in front of a judge, but it also applies to the judge who turns justice into injustice and vice versa by manipulating the legal system. In such a case, the judge is giving false testimony every bit as much as a witness can. The same is true of any person who makes the straight seem crooked and the crooked straight, and it is likewise true of any religious authority who distorts what is true in the Word and perverts its goodness.

To put it briefly, any distortion of the truth from a bad motive is false testimony, whether on the spiritual level or on the level of morality and citizenship.

1020. [2] When we resist giving false testimony, whether in a moral or spiritual sense, and avoid it and reject it as sinful, a desire to be truthful and just flows into us from the Lord through heaven. When as a result we love truthfulness and justice, we are loving the Lord, because he is truthfulness and justice itself.

When we love being truthful and just, truthfulness and justice can be said to love us, because the Lord loves us. Then our voice becomes the voice of truthfulness, and our endeavors become the works of justice.

The Ninth Commandment
You Shall Not Covet Your Neighbor's House

1021. [2] All coveting, or craving, comes from twin loves called worldly ambition and self-love, which are like streams gushing from their sources and flowing on endlessly. Craving is our love's constant urge, because when we love something, we constantly long for it. If it comes from love of evil, we call it craving; but if it comes from love of good, we call it desire or affection.

Worldly ambition and self-love are the sources of every kind of craving. Since all types of evil craving are forbidden by these last two commandments, it make sense that the ninth commandment would forbid craving that springs from worldly ambition and that the tenth would forbid craving that springs from self-love.

Not coveting another person's house means not craving their property—their possessions and wealth—and not taking it for ourselves by devious methods. This craving comes from worldly ambition.

✄   ✄   ✄

The Tenth Commandment
You Shall Not Covet (or Pursue) Your Friend's Wife, His Male Servant or Female Servant, His Ox, or His Donkey

1022. [2] This means craving the things that a person identifies with himself or herself most strongly. Since the *wife, servant, maid, ox*, and *donkey* are within our household, on the inner, spiritual level of meaning these things within our household are aspects of our self-identity. Specifically, *wife* means our passion for truth and goodness on a spiritual level; *male servant* and *female servant* mean passion for truth and goodness on a rational level, in support of our spiritual passion; and *ox* and *donkey* mean passion for truth and goodness on an earthly level. In the Word, *wife, male servant, female servant, ox*, and *donkey* symbolize these kinds of passion.

Craving or being greedy for such passions [in other people] means really wanting to subject them to our power and bring them under our control. Craving their passion [for truth and goodness] is the craving of our self-love, that is, our desire to control them. In this way, we claim for ourselves the identity of the people with whom we associate.

[3] All of this demonstrates that the craving of the ninth commandment is a craving that comes from worldly ambition, and the craving of this tenth commandment is a craving that comes from self-love. As I said before, all cravings come from love, because it is love that desires; and since every craving is associated with these twin evil loves, self-love and worldly ambition, it is only logical that the craving of the ninth commandment pertains to worldly ambition and the craving of this commandment pertains to self-love, especially the desire to control other people.

⚜ ⚜ ⚜

About the Ten Commandments in General

1024. [2] The commandments of the Decalogue are called the *Ten Words* or Ten Commandments, because *ten* means all; and so in this context, *Ten Words* means a summary of everything in the Word; and by extension, it means anything that relates to the church.

The Ten Commandments are able to summarize everything the Word and the church teach, because there are three levels of meaning within each commandment. Each level of meaning is suited to its own heaven, of which there are three. The first level of meaning is the spiritual-moral meaning and is suited to the first, or outermost, heaven; the second is the heavenly-spiritual meaning and is suited to the second, or middle, heaven; and the third is the divine-heavenly meaning and is suited to the third, or inmost, heaven. Everything in the Word has these three inner meanings, because the Word was sent down from the Lord on high through the three heavens successively, until it reached this earth. In this way, it was accommodated to each heaven, and so each heaven and practically each angel has the Word at the appropriate level of meaning. The angels read it daily and draw their sermons from it, just as we do in our world.

[3] The Word is actually the divine truth (and therefore the divine wisdom), and it comes forth from the Lord as [light] comes from the sun. In heaven, it appears as light. Divine truth is that divine entity we call the Holy Spirit. It not only comes forth from the Lord, but it enlightens people and teaches them, as we say of the Holy Spirit. As it descends from the Lord, the Word is accommodated to the three heavens; and just as the three heavens are interconnected, with the innermost being connected to the outermost by means of the intermediate, the three levels of the Word's meaning are joined in the same fashion.

It is obvious, then, that the Word exists to connect the heavens with each other and to connect them with the human race, for whom a literal meaning is provided, which is purely earthly and therefore is a foundation for the other three levels of meaning.

The only way to understand how the Ten Commandments summarize everything in the Word is to look at the commandments in these three levels of meaning as I have described them.

⚜ ⚜ ⚜

1025. [2] From the following brief explanation, one can understand the nature of these three levels of meaning in the Ten Commandments. The spiritual-moral meaning of the first commandment, *you shall not worship other gods before* *me*, involves not worshipping anything or anyone else as divine; for example, not worshipping nature by giving it some divine attribute of its own or not worshipping some representative of the Lord or a saint.

The heavenly-spiritual meaning involves acknowledging only one God, not many gods according to their attributes (as the ancient peoples did and some non-Christians do today) or according to their powers (as do those Christians today who have one god as the creator, one as the redeemer, and one as the enlightener).

The divine-heavenly meaning of this same commandment involves acknowledging and worshipping the Lord alone and only within him these three natures: the divine one from eternity, meant by the *Father;* the divine human born within time, meant by the *Son of God*; and the divinity that comes from these two, meant by the *Holy Spirit.*

These are the three successive levels of meaning in the first commandment. It is obvious from looking at this commandment in its threefold meaning that it comprehensively contains everything specifically having to do with the deity's essence, in summary form.

[4] In its three levels of meaning, the second commandment, *you shall not profane the name of God*, comprehensively contains everything that specifically relates to the character of the deity. *The name of God* means his character; and in the first level of meaning, that is the Word, the teachings from the Word, and the religious practice that comes from those teachings in terms of what we say and what we do. The second level of meaning is about the Lord's kingdom, both in this world and in heaven. The third level of meaning is about the Lord's divine human aspect, because this is what holiness in its essence really is. (In *Revelation Explained* 224, you may see how the highest meaning of *the name of God* is the Lord's

divine human aspect.) In the rest of the commandments, there are likewise three inner levels of meaning that represent the three heavens. I will write about them at another time, the Lord willing.

⚹ ⚹ ⚹

1026. [3] Divine truth united with divine goodness comes forth from the Lord as [heat and light come] from the sun, and this is what created heaven and the world (John 1:1, 3, 10). This is why everything in heaven and the world relate to what is good and true: anything that happens or is created is the result of the combination of these two. The Ten Commandments contain everything that has to do with divine goodness and divine truth and also how the two combine.

How divine truth and divine goodness come together in the Ten Commandments is mysterious. It is something like the joining together of love for the Lord and love toward other people: divine love relates to love for the Lord, and divine truth relates to love toward other people. When we live according to divine truth, that is, love other people, then the Lord flows into us with divine goodness and joins himself with us.

This is why the Ten Commandments were written upon matching tablets of stone and why they were called a *covenant*, which means a joining together. They were placed in the ark, not side by side but one on top of the other, as evidence of the connection between the Lord and us. The commandments teaching us to love the Lord were written upon one tablet, and the commandments teaching us to love our neighbor were written upon the other. The first three commandments teach us to love the Lord; the last six teach us to love the neighbor; and the fourth, *honor your father and your mother*, is a bridge commandment, since in heaven *father* means the Lord and *mother* means the church, which is the neighbor.

⚜ ⚜ ⚜

1027. [2] Now I should say something about how this connection between God and us is brought into effect by means of the precepts in the Ten Commandments. The Lord alone joins us with himself; we do not join ourselves with the Lord. The Lord joins us with himself in the following manner: we learn about the commandments, come to understand them, want to obey them, and then obey them. The connection happens when we obey them. If, on the other hand, we do not obey them, we stop wanting to obey them—and ultimately cease to understand them and learn about them. After all, what does it mean to want to obey the commandments if we do not obey them when we have the chance? Is it a mere abstraction? The logical assumption, then, is that the connection happens when we obey the precepts in the Ten Commandments.

[3] I have said that the Lord alone joins us to himself, and that we do not join ourselves to the Lord, and that the connection happens when the commandments are obeyed. This means the Lord obeys the commandments on our behalf, and yet anyone can see that a covenant cannot be entered into and a conjunction take place unless there is some reciprocation on our part so that we not only give our consent but take ownership. To this end, the Lord endows us with the freedom to decide what we want and to act on it as though we are doing it independently. The nature of this freedom is that as far as we know, when we are thinking about the truth or doing something good, we believe it is happening inside us and therefore that we are doing it ourselves. We have this reciprocation so that conjunction can take place; yet because this

freedom comes from the Lord and is constantly maintained by him, we should fully acknowledge that when we are pondering and understanding the truth, wanting to do good things, and doing them, it is not being done by us but by the Lord, as I explained on this subject in *Revelation Explained* 946, 971, and 973.

[4] When we join with the Lord by obeying the six final commandments as though doing it on our own, then the Lord joins with us by means of the first three commandments: that we should acknowledge God, believe in the Lord, and consider his name holy. We are not following these three commandments in good faith, no matter how much we think we are, unless we are resisting because they are sins the wrongdoings specified in the six final commandments on the second tablet. The commandments constitute a covenant on the Lord's part and on our part. By means of them, a reciprocal conjunction takes place so that we can be within the Lord and the Lord within us (John 14:20).

❧ ❧ ❧

1028. [2] Some say that sinning against one of the Ten Commandments is sinning against all of them and that if you are guilty of one, you are guilty of them all. Let me explain the truth of this statement. Those who violate one commandment, convincing themselves it is not a sin and committing the act without a fear of God, are not afraid to violate all of the commandments (even if they do not actually do so), precisely because they have abandoned their fear of God.

[3] For example, people who commit fraud or embezzlement, which are essentially theft, and do not consider it sin will likewise not consider it sinful to commit adultery with another man's wife, to hate him enough to kill him, to slander him, or to crave his house or the other things he owns. Those

who intentionally disregard God in the case of one commandment are denying that anything is sinful. At that point, they associate with people who violate the rest of the commandments without regard for God. Like infernal spirits in a hell of thieves, they may not be adulterers, murderers, or perjurers, but still they can be convinced by their associates that these things are not bad and can be persuaded to do them. Once they have become infernal spirits by violating one commandment, they no longer believe it is sinful to do anything against God or against other people.

[4] The opposite is true for those who resist the evil in any one of the commandments, who flee it and reject it as a sin against God. Because they are mindful of God, they associate with the angels of heaven; and the Lord leads them to refrain from the evils in the rest of the commandments and to avoid them and eventually reject them because they are sinful. And if they should happen to sin against those commandments, they promptly do penance; and in this way, they are gradually withdrawn from those sins.

—◆—

Life (1763)

≈

The Ten Commandments Tell Us Which Evils Are Sins

53. Is there any society anywhere on the globe that does not know that it is evil to steal, commit adultery, murder, and bear false witness? If they did not know this, and if they were not prevented by laws from doing these things, it would be all over for them, because any community or republic or kingdom would collapse if it did not have these laws. Could anyone presume that the Israelite nation was so much more stupid than everyone else that they did not know these things were evil? So we might wonder why these laws, so well known over the whole face of the earth, were made public by Jehovah himself from Mount Sinai in such miraculous fashion.

But the truth is that they were made public in such miraculous fashion to let Israel know that these laws are not merely civil and moral laws but are spiritual laws as well, and that breaking them is not only harmful to our fellow citizens and communities but is also a sin against God. So the proclamation of these laws from Mount Sinai by Jehovah made them laws of religion. It is obvious that if Jehovah God commands something, he does so in order to make it a part of our religion, as something that needs to be done for his sake and for the sake of our own salvation.

54. Because these laws were the very beginnings of the Word and therefore of the church that the Lord was establishing with the Israelite people, and because they brought together in a brief summary all the elements of religion that make possible the Lord's union with us and our union with the Lord, they were so holy that nothing is holier.

55. We can tell how supremely holy they were from the fact that Jehovah himself—the Lord, that is—came down upon Mount Sinai in fire, with angels, and proclaimed them from there with his own voice, and that the people spent three days preparing themselves for seeing and hearing all this. The mountain was also fenced off so that no one would approach it and die. Not even priests or elders were allowed near; Moses alone was allowed. The laws were written on two stone tablets by the finger of God. When Moses brought the tablets down from the mountain the second time, his face shone. Later they were placed in an ark, which was set in the very heart of the tabernacle and had a mercy seat on it, with angel guardians made of gold above that. There was nothing holier in their church, and it was called "the most holy place." Outside the veil that surrounded it they brought together things that represented holy elements of heaven and the church—the lampstand with its seven golden lamps, the golden altar of incense, and the gilded table for the showbread, all surrounded by curtains of fine linen and purple and scarlet thread. The sole reason for the holiness of this whole tabernacle was the law that was in the ark.

[2] Because of the holiness of the tabernacle, which resulted from the presence of the law in the ark, the whole Israelite population camped around it, in a set arrangement tribe by tribe, and traveled behind it in a set sequence. There was also

a cloud above it in the daytime then, and fire above it at night. Because of the holiness of the law and the Lord's presence in it, it was upon the mercy seat between the angel guardians that the Lord spoke to Moses, and the ark was called "Jehovah" there. In fact Aaron was not allowed to go behind the veil without sacrifices and incense.

Because the law was the essential holiness of the church, David brought the ark into Zion, and it was later placed at the center of the Jerusalem temple where [Solomon] had made an inner sanctuary for it.

[3] Because of the Lord's presence in and around the law, miracles were performed by means of the ark in which the law lay. For example, the waters of the Jordan were cut off, and as long as the ark rested in its midst, the people crossed over on dry ground. The walls of Jericho fell because the ark was carried around them. Dagon, the god of the Philistines, fell before the ark and later lay on the threshold of the shrine with its head broken off. Tens of thousands of the people of Beth-shemesh were struck down because of the ark, and so on. All these things happened simply because of the Lord's presence in his *Ten Words*, which are the Ten Commandments.

56. Another reason for the power and holiness of that law is that it is a summary of everything that constitutes religion. That is, it consisted of two tablets, one briefly containing everything that has to do with God and the other everything that has to do with us. That is why the commandments of that law are called the *Ten Words*—so called because *ten* means all.

How that law summarizes everything that constitutes religion, though, will be explained under the next heading [§64].

57. Because that law is the means of the Lord's union with us and our union with the Lord, it is called a *covenant* and a *testimony*—a covenant because it unites and a testimony because it bears witness.

That is why there were two tablets, one for the Lord and one for us. The union is effected by the Lord, but it is effected when we do what is written on our tablet. That is, the Lord is constantly present and active and wanting to come in, but because of the freedom he gives us, it is up to us to open [the door], for he says,

> Behold, I stand at the door and knock. If any hear my voice and open the door, I will come in to them and dine with them and they with me. (Revelation 3:20)

58. In the second tablet, which is for us, it does not say that we must do some specific good thing but that we must not do some specific evil thing—for example, *You are not to kill, you are not to commit adultery, you are not to steal, you are not to bear false witness, you are not to covet.* This is because we cannot do anything good on our own, but when we do not do evil things, the good things we do come not from ourselves but from the Lord.

We shall see in what follows [§§101–107] that we can turn our backs on evil—seemingly on our own, but actually with the Lord's power—if we ask for this humbly. . . .

61. The commandments of the law were called the *Ten Words* (Exodus 34:28; Deuteronomy 4:13; 10:4). This is because *ten* means all and *words* means truths. After all, there were more than ten.

Because *ten* means all, there were ten curtains of the tabernacle (Exodus 26:1). That is why the Lord said that the one who was going to receive a kingdom called ten servants and gave them ten minas for doing business (Luke 19:13). It is why the Lord compared the kingdom of the heavens to ten young women (Matthew 25:1), and why the dragon is described as having ten horns (Revelation 12:3). The same holds true for the beast rising up out of the sea (Revelation 13:1), and the other beast (Revelation 17:3, 7), as well as the beast in Daniel (Daniel 7:7, 20, 24). *Ten* means the same in Leviticus 26:26, Zechariah 8:23, and elsewhere.

That is where *tithes* come from, meaning some portion of all.

All Kinds of Murder, Adultery, Theft, and False Witness, Together with Urges toward Them, Are Evils on Which We Must Turn Our Backs Because They Are Sins

62. It is common knowledge that the law of Sinai was written on two tablets and that the first tablet contains matters concerning God and the second, matters concerning us. It is not obvious in the literal text that the first tablet contains everything to do with God and that the second contains everything to do with us, but it is all in there. It is actually why they are called the *Ten Words*, meaning all truths in summary (see §61 just above). However, there is no way to explain briefly how everything is there, though it can be grasped by reference to what is presented in §67 of *Sacred Scripture*, which the reader may consult.

This is the reason for mentioning "*all kinds* of murder, adultery, theft, and false witness."

63. The prevailing religious belief holds that no one can fulfill the law. And [yet] the law demands that we must not kill, commit adultery, steal, or bear false witness. Any civic and moral individual can fulfill these elements of the law by living a good civic and moral life; but this religious belief denies that we can do so by living a good spiritual life. This leads to the conclusion that our reason for not committing these crimes is simply to avoid punishment and loss in this world, but not to avoid punishment and loss after we leave this world. The result is that people who hold this conviction think that immoral actions are permissible in the eyes of God but not in the eyes of the world.

[2] Because of the kind of thinking that is based on this religious principle, people have cravings to commit all these evils; for worldly reasons only, they forgo doing them. So even if they have not committed murder, adultery, theft, or false witness, after death people like this still feel the urge to commit such sins; and they actually do when they lose the outer façade they had in the world. All our cravings await us after death. This is why people like this act in concert with hell and cannot help suffering the same fate as people in hell.

[3] Things turn out differently, though, if we do not want to murder, commit adultery, steal, or bear false witness, because such behavior is contrary to God. Once we have fought against them to some extent we do not intend them, so we feel no urge to do them. We say in our hearts that they are sins, essentially hellish and diabolic. Then after death, when we lose any façade we maintained for worldly reasons, we act in concert with heaven; and because we are focused on the Lord, we also enter heaven.

64. Every religion has the general principle that we are to examine ourselves, practice repentance, and refrain from sins, and if we do not do this, we suffer damnation. (See *Life* 1–8 on this being a common feature of all religion.)

The whole Christian world also has the common practice of teaching the Ten Commandments as a way of introducing little children to the Christian religion. These commandments are in every little child's hand. Their parents and teachers tell them that doing such things is sinning against God. In fact, when they talk with children they have no other thought in their heads but this. It is little short of amazing that these same people, and the children when they grow up, think that they are not subject to the law and that they are incapable of doing what the law requires. Can there be any reason why they learn to think like this other than that they love evils and therefore love the false notions that support them? These are the individuals, then, who do not regard the Ten Commandments as matters of religion. See *Faith* on the fact that there is no religion in the lives of such people.

65. Every society on the face of the whole earth that has any religion has laws like the Ten Commandments, and all the individuals who live by them as a matter of religion are saved, while all who do not live by them as a matter of religion are damned. After death, the ones who have lived by them as a matter of religion are taught by angels, accept truths, and acknowledge the Lord. This is because they have turned their backs on evils because they are sins and have therefore been devoted to doing what is good, and their resulting goodness loves truth and eagerly drinks it in (see *Life* 32–41).

This is the meaning of the Lord's words to the Jews:

> The kingdom of God will be taken from you and given to a nation that bears fruit. (Matthew 21:43)

And also these words:

> When the lord of the vineyard comes, he will destroy those evil people and lease his vineyard to other farmers who will give him its fruits in their season. (Matthew 21:40, 41)

And these:

> I tell you that many will come from the east and the west, and from the north and the south, and will sit down in the kingdom of God, but the children of the kingdom will be cast out into outer darkness. (Matthew 8:11, 12; Luke 13:29)

66. We read in Mark that a certain rich man came to Jesus and asked him what he needed to do in order to inherit eternal life. Jesus said, "You know the commandments: you are not to commit adultery; you are not to kill; you are not to steal; you are not to bear false witness; you are not to commit fraud; honor your father and mother." He replied, "Since my youth I have kept all these things." Jesus looked at him and loved him, but said, "One thing you lack: Go, sell whatever you have and give to the poor, and you will have treasure in the heavens; and come, take up the cross, and follow me" (Mark 10:17–22).

[2] It says that Jesus loved him, and this was because he had kept the commandments since his youth. Because he lacked three things, though—he had not detached his heart from wealth, he had not fought against his cravings, and he had not yet acknowledged the Lord as God—the Lord told him that he was to sell everything he had, meaning that he was to detach his heart from wealth; that he was to take up the cross, meaning that he was to fight against his cravings; and that he was to follow him, meaning that he was to acknowledge the Lord as God. The Lord said these things the way he said everything else—in correspondences (see *Sacred Scripture* 17). The fact is that we—and this means everyone—cannot turn our backs on evils because they are sins unless we acknowledge the Lord and turn to him, and unless we fight against evils, and in this way distance ourselves from our cravings.

More on this, though, under the heading concerning doing battle against evils [§§92–99].

To the Extent That We Turn Our Backs on All Kinds of Killing Because They Are Sins, We Have Love for Our Neighbor

67. *All kinds of killing* means all kinds of hostility, hatred, and vengefulness, which yearn for murder. Killing lies hidden

within such attitudes like fire that smolders beneath the ashes. That is exactly what hellfire is. It is why we say that people are on fire with hatred and burning for vengeance. These are types of killing in an earthly sense; but in a spiritual sense *killing* means all of the many and varied ways of killing and destroying people's souls. Then in the highest sense it means harboring hatred for the Lord.

These three kinds of killing align and are united, since anyone who intends the physical murder of someone in this world intends the murder of that individual's soul after death and intends the murder of the Lord, actually burning with hatred against him and wanting to eradicate his name.

68. These kinds of killing lie hidden within us from birth, but from early childhood we learn to veil them with the civility and morality we need when we are with others in this world; and to the extent that we yearn for rank or money, we take care not to let them become visible. This latter character becomes our outside, while the former is our inside and is what we are like in and of ourselves; so you can see how demonic we will be after death, when we put off that outside along with our bodies, unless we have been reformed.

69. Since the kinds of killing just mentioned lie hidden within us from birth, as noted, along with all kinds of theft and all kinds of false witness and the urges to commit them (which will be described shortly [§§80–86, 87–91]), we can see that if the Lord had not provided means of reformation, we would inevitably perish forever.

The means of reformation that the Lord has provided are the following: we are born into utter ignorance; as newborns we are kept in a state of outward innocence; soon thereafter we are kept in a state of outward goodwill and then in a state of outward friendship. But as we become capable of thinking with our own intellect, we are kept in some freedom to act rationally. This is the state described in *Life* 19, and I need to turn back to it at this point for the sake of what will follow.

As long as we are in this world we are in between hell and heaven—hell is below us and heaven above us—and during this time we are kept in a freedom to turn toward hell or toward heaven. If we turn toward hell we are turning away from heaven, while if we turn toward heaven we are turning away from hell.

In other words, as long as we are in this world we are placed in between the Lord and the Devil and are kept in a freedom to turn toward the one or the other. If we turn toward the Devil we turn our backs on the Lord, while if we turn toward the Lord we turn our backs on the Devil.

Or to put it yet another way, as long as we are in this world we are in between what is evil and what is good and are kept in a freedom to turn toward the one or the other. If we turn toward what is evil we turn our backs on what is good, while if we turn toward what is good we turn our backs on what is evil.

This you will find in §19; see also §§20, 21, and 22, which follow it.

70. Now, since what is evil and what is good are two opposite things, like hell and heaven or like the Devil and the Lord, it follows that if we turn our backs on something evil as a sin we come into something good that is the opposite of that evil. The goodness that is opposite to the evil meant by killing is loving our neighbor.

71. Since this goodness and that evil are opposites, it follows that the latter is repelled by the former. Two opposites cannot be one, as heaven and hell cannot be one. If they did, it would be like that lukewarm state described in the book of Revelation as follows:

I know that you are neither cold nor hot. It would have been better if you were cold or hot; but since you are lukewarm and neither cold nor hot, I am about to vomit you out of my mouth. (Revelation 3:15, 16)

72. When we are no longer caught up in the evil of killing but are moved by the good we do out of love for our neighbor, then whatever we do is something good that results from that love, so it is a good work. Priests who are engaged in this goodness are doing a good work whenever they teach and lead because it comes from a love for saving souls. People in administrative roles who are engaged in this goodness are doing a good work whenever they make arrangements and decisions because it comes from a love for serving the country, the community, and their fellow citizens. By the same token, if merchants are engaged in this goodness all of their business is a good work. There is love for their neighbor within it, and their neighbor is the country, the community, their fellow citizens, and their own households as well, whose well-being concerns them as much as their own does. Laborers who are devoted to this goodness do their work faithfully because of it, acting as much for others as for themselves, and being as fearful of harming others as of harming themselves.

The reason their actions are good deeds is that to the extent that we turn our backs on anything evil we do something good, in keeping with the general principle presented in *Life* 21; and anyone who turns away from something evil as a sin is doing what is good not because of his or her self but because of the Lord (see *Life* 18–31).

On the contrary, if we do not regard all kinds of killing—hostility, hatred, vengeance, and the like—as sins, then whether we are priests, administrators, merchants, or laborers, no matter what we do it is not a good deed, because everything we do shares in the evil that is within it. It is in fact what is inside that is producing it. The outside may be good, but only for others, not for ourselves.

73. The Lord teaches good and loving actions in many passages in the Word. He teaches such actions in Matthew when he instructs us to be reconciled with our neighbor:

> If you bring your gift to the altar and in doing so remember that your brother or sister has something against you, leave your gift there in front of the altar. First be reconciled with your brother or sister, and then come and offer your gift. And be kind and generous to your adversary when you are both on the way [to court], to keep your adversary from turning you over to a judge, keep the judge from turning you over to an officer, and keep you from being thrown in prison. I tell you in truth, you will not be released until you have paid the last penny. (Matthew 5:23–26)

Being reconciled with our brother or sister is turning our backs on hostility, hatred, and vengefulness. We can see that this is turning our backs on these evils because they are sins.

The Lord also tells us in Matthew,

> Whatever you want people to do for you, you do the same for them. This is the Law and the Prophets. (Matthew 7:12)

[We should do] nothing evil, then; and [this is said] quite often elsewhere. Then too, the Lord tells us that killing is also being angry with our sister or brother or neighbor for no good reason and harboring hatred against them (see Matthew 5:21, 22).

To the Extent That We Turn Our Backs on All Kinds of Adultery Because They Are Sins, We Love Chastity

74. Understood on an earthly level, the adultery named in the sixth commandment means not only acts of fornication but also lecherous behavior, lewd conversation, and filthy thoughts. Understood on a spiritual level, though, adultery

means polluting what is good in the Word and distorting what is true in it, while understood on the highest level it means denying the divine nature of the Lord and profaning the Word. These are *all kinds of adultery*.

On the basis of rational light, earthly-minded people can know that *adultery* also means lecherous behavior, lewd conversation, and filthy thoughts, but not that adultery means polluting what is good in the Word and distorting what is true in it, and certainly not that it means denying the divine nature of the Lord and profaning the Word. So they do not know that adultery is so evil that it can be called the height of wickedness. This is because anyone who is intent on earthly adultery is also intent on spiritual adultery, and the reverse. This will be shown in a separate booklet on marriage. But in fact, people whose faith and way of life do not lead them to regard adultery as a sin are engaged in the totality of adultery at every moment.

75. The reason people love marriage to the extent that they turn their backs on adultery—or to be more precise, love the chastity of marriage to the extent that they turn their backs on the lechery of adultery—is that the lechery of adultery and the chastity of marriage are two opposite things. This means that to the extent that we are not intent on the one we are intent on the other. This is exactly like what has been said in §70 above.

76. We cannot know the true nature of the chastity of marriage if we do not turn our backs on the lechery of adultery as a sin. We can know something we have experienced, but not something that we have not experienced. If we know about something we have not experienced, know it on the basis of a description or by thinking about it, we know it only in the shadows, and doubt clings to it. So we see it in the light and without doubt only when we have experienced it. This is knowing, then; the other is knowing and yet not knowing.

The truth of the matter is that the lechery of adultery and the chastity of marriage are as different from each other as hell and heaven are from each other, and that the lechery of adultery makes hell for us and the chastity of marriage makes heaven for us.

However, there is no chastity of marriage for anyone but those who turn their backs on adultery as a sin—see §111 below.

77. This enables us to conclude and see beyond doubt whether someone is a Christian or not, in fact whether or not someone has any religion at all. People who do not regard adultery as a sin in their faith and their way of life are not Christians and have no religion. On the other hand, people who turn their backs on adultery as a sin, and more so people who steer clear of it altogether for that reason, and even more so people who detest it for that reason, do have a religion, and if they are in the Christian church, they are Christians.

There will be more on this in the booklet on marriage, though; and in the meanwhile those interested may consult what it says on this subject in *Heaven and Hell* 366–386.

78. We can tell from what the Lord says in Matthew that adultery also means lecherous behavior, lewd conversation, and filthy thoughts:

> You have heard that it was said by the ancients, "You are not to commit adultery"; but I tell you that anyone who has looked at someone else's wife in order to desire her has already committed adultery with her in his heart. (Matthew 5:27, 28)

79. The following passages show that spiritually understood, *adultery* means polluting what is good in the Word and distorting what is true in it:

> Babylon has made all nations drink of the wine of her fornication. (Revelation 14:8)

An angel said, "I will show you the judgment of the great whore who sits on many waters, with whom the kings of the earth committed fornication." (Revelation 17:1, 2)

Babylon has made all nations drink of the wine of the wrath of her fornication, and the kings of the earth have committed fornication with her. (Revelation 18:3)

God has judged the great whore who corrupted the earth with her fornication. (Revelation 19:2)

Fornication is associated with Babylon because Babylon means people who claim the Lord's divine power for themselves and profane the Word by polluting and distorting it. That is why Babylon is called the *Mother of Fornications and of the Abominations of the Earth* in Revelation 17:5.

[2] *Fornication* means much the same in the prophets—in Jeremiah, for example:

In the prophets of Jerusalem I have seen appalling obstinacy; they commit adultery and walk in a lie. (Jeremiah 23:14)

In Ezekiel:

Two women, daughters of one mother, played the whore in Egypt; in their youth they behaved wantonly. The first was unfaithful to me and took delight in lovers from neighboring Assyria. Upon them, too, she bestowed her acts of whoredom, but without giving up her wantonness in Egypt. The second became more corrupt in her love than the first, and her acts of whoredom were worse than her sister's. She increased her whoredom and made love to Chaldeans; sons of Babel came to her, into the bed of love, and defiled her with their debauchery. (Ezekiel 23:2–17)

This is about the church of Israel and Judah, who are the *daughters of one mother* in this passage. Their *acts of whoredom* mean their pollutions and distortions of the Word, and since in the Word *Egypt* means factual knowledge, *Assyria* reasoning, *Chaldea* the profanation of what is true, and *Babel* the profanation of what is good, it says that they committed acts of whoredom with those countries. . . .

To the Extent That We Turn Our Backs on All Kinds of Theft Because They Are Sins, We Love Honesty

80. In earthly terms, *theft* means not only theft and robbery but also cheating and taking other people's assets by some pretext. Spiritually understood, though, *theft* means depriving others of the truths of their faith and good actions motivated by their goodwill, while in the highest sense it means taking from the Lord what is properly his and claiming it for ourselves—that is, claiming righteousness and worth for ourselves. These are *all kinds of theft*, and like *all kinds of adultery* and *all kinds of killing*, as just described [§§74–79 and §§67–73], they too are united. They are united because one is within the other.

81. The evil of theft infects us more deeply than some other evils because it is united with guile and trickery, and guile and trickery work their way into our spiritual mind where our thinking with understanding takes place. We shall see below that we have a spiritual mind and an earthly mind [§86].

82. The reason we love honesty to the extent that we turn our backs on theft as a sin is that theft is also deception, and deception and honesty are two opposite things. This means that to the extent that we are not devoted to deception, we are devoted to honesty.

83. *Honesty* also means integrity, fairness, faithfulness, and morality. On our own, we cannot be devoted to these so as to love them for what they are, for their own sakes, but if we turn our backs on deception, guile, and trickery as sins, we have a devotion to these virtues that comes not from ourselves but from the Lord, as explained in *Life* 18–31. This applies to priests, administrators, judges, merchants, and laborers—to all of us then, in our various roles and tasks.

84. There are many passages in the Word that say this, the following being a few of them:

> Those who walk in righteousness and say what is upright, who loathe oppression for the sake of profit, who shake bribes from their hands in order not to accept them, who block their ears so as not to hear bloodshed, who close their eyes so as not to see evil—they will dwell on high. (Isaiah 33:15, 16)

> Jehovah, who will dwell in your tabernacle? Who will live on your holy mountain? Those who walk uprightly and do what is fair, who do not disparage others with their tongues, and who do no evil to their companions. (Psalms 15:1, 2, 3, and following)

> My eyes are toward the faithful of the earth so that they may sit down with me. Anyone who walks the path of integrity will serve me. No one who practices deceit will sit in the midst of my house; no one who speaks lies will stand in my presence. At dawn I will cut off all the ungodly of the earth, to cut off from the city all those who work iniquity. (Psalms 101:6, 7, 8)

[2] In the following words, the Lord tells us that we are not truly honest, fair, faithful, or upright until we are inwardly honest, fair, faithful, and upright:

> Unless your righteousness exceeds that of the scribes and Pharisees, you will not enter the kingdom of the heavens. (Matthew 5:20)

Righteousness that exceeds that of the scribes and Pharisees means the more inward righteousness that is ours when we are in the Lord. As for our being *in the Lord*, he also teaches this in John:

> The glory that you gave me I have given them, so that they may be one just as we are one—I in them and you in me—so that they may be made perfect in one, and so that the love with which you loved me may be in them, and I may be in them. (John 17:22, 23, 26)

This shows that people become complete when the Lord is in them. These are the people who are called *pure in heart*, the ones who *will see God*, and the ones who are *perfect, like their Father in the heavens* (Matthew 5:8, 48).

85. I noted in §81 above that the evil of theft infects us more deeply than some other evils because it is united with guile and trickery, and guile and trickery work their way into our spiritual mind where our thinking with understanding takes place; so now I need to say something about the human *mind*. On the human mind being our understanding together with our will, see *Life* 43.

86. We have an earthly mind and a spiritual mind, the earthly mind below and the spiritual mind above. The earthly mind is our mind for this world and the spiritual mind is our mind for heaven. The earthly mind can be called the animal mind, while the spiritual mind can be called the human mind. We are differentiated from animals by our having a spiritual mind that makes it possible for us to be in heaven while we are in this world. It is also what makes it possible for us to live after death.

[2] We can use our faculty of understanding to be in the spiritual side of our mind, and thus to be in heaven, but we cannot use our faculty of willing to be so unless we turn our backs on evils because they are sins; and if our will is not in heaven as well [as our understanding], we ourselves are still not there, because our will drags our understanding back down and makes it just as earthly and animal as itself.

[3] We can be compared to a garden, our understanding to light, and our will to warmth. A garden has light in winter but no warmth, while it has both light and warmth in summer. So when all we have is the light of our understanding, we are like a garden in winter, but when we have both light in our understanding and warmth in our will we are like a garden in summer.

In fact, the wisdom in our understanding comes from spiritual light and the love in our will comes from spiritual warmth, for spiritual light is divine wisdom and spiritual warmth is divine love.

[4] If we fail to turn our backs on evils because they are sins, the cravings of our evils clog the deeper levels of our earthly mind on the side where our will resides and are like a thick veil, like black clouds beneath the spiritual mind, preventing it from opening. However, as soon as we turn our backs on evils because they are sins, the Lord flows in from heaven, takes the veil away, dispels the cloud, and opens the spiritual mind, thereby admitting us to heaven.

[5] As already noted, as long as cravings for evil behavior clog the deeper levels of the earthly mind, we are in hell, but as soon as those cravings are dispelled by the Lord, we are in heaven. Again, as long as cravings for evil behavior clog the deeper levels of the earthly mind we are earthly people, but as soon as those cravings are dispelled by the Lord, we are spiritual people. Again, as long as cravings for evil behavior clog the deeper levels of the earthly mind we are animals, differing from them only in that we are capable of thinking and talking, even about things we cannot see with our eyes (we can do this because of the ability of our understanding to be lifted up into heaven's light). As soon as those cravings have been dispelled by the Lord, though, we are human because we are thinking what is true in our understanding because of what

is good in our will. And yet again, as long as cravings for evil behavior clog the deeper levels of the earthly mind we are like a garden in winter, but as soon as those cravings are dispelled by the Lord, we are like a garden in summer.

[6] In the Word, the union of our will and understanding is meant by *heart and soul* and by *heart and spirit*, as when it says that we are "to love God with all our heart and with all our soul" (Matthew 22:37) and that God will give "a new heart and a new spirit" (Ezekiel 11:19; 36:26, 27). Our *heart* means our will and its love, while our *soul* or *spirit* means our understanding and its wisdom.

To the Extent That We Turn Our Backs on All Kinds of False Witness Because They Are Sins, We Love Truth

87. Understood on an earthly level, bearing false witness means not only committing legal perjury but also telling lies and slandering others. Understood on a spiritual level, bearing false witness means saying and convincing ourselves that something false is true and that something evil is good, and the reverse. Understood on the highest level, though, bearing false witness means blaspheming the Lord and the Word. These are the three meanings of false witness.

The information about the threefold meaning of everything in the Word presented in *Sacred Scripture* 5, 6, 7, and following may show that these three are united in people who commit perjury, tell lies, and slander.

88. Since lying and truth are two opposite things, it follows that to the extent that we turn our backs on lying because it is a sin, we love truth.

89. To the extent that we love truth we want to know it and we find our hearts moved when we find it. That is the only way to arrive at wisdom; and to the extent that we love to do the truth, we take pleasure in the light that contains it.

This is the same as in the case of the commandments already discussed, such as honesty and fairness in those who turn their backs on all kinds of theft, chastity and purity in those who turn their backs on all kinds of adultery, love and caring in those who turn their backs on all kinds of killing, and so on.

People who are caught up in the opposite attitudes, though, know nothing about all this, even though it involves everything that is actually anything.

90. *Truth* is meant by the seed in the field, which the Lord described as follows:

> A sower went out to sow seed. As he was sowing, some seed fell on a much-trodden path, and the birds of heaven devoured it. Some seed fell on stony places, but as soon as it grew up it withered, because it had no root. Some seed fell among thorns, and the thorns grew up with it and choked it. And some seed fell on good ground, and when it grew up it bore abundant fruit. (Luke 8:5–8; Matthew 13:3–8; Mark 4:3–8)

In this parable the sower is the Lord and the seed is his Word and therefore the truth. The seed on the path refers to the way the Word is viewed by people who do not care about truth. The seed in stony places refers to the way the Word is viewed by people who do care about truth, but not for its own sake, and therefore not deeply. The seed among thorns refers to the way the Word is viewed by people who are caught up in cravings for evil behavior, while the seed in good ground is the way the Word is viewed by people who love the truths that come from the Lord and are found in the Word, the people who bear fruit because their doing of those truths comes from him. We are assured of these meanings by the Lord's explanation (Matthew 13:19–23, 37; Mark 4:14–20; Luke 8:11–15).

We can see from this that the truth of the Word cannot take root in people who do not care about truth or in people who love truth superficially but not deeply or in people who are caught up in cravings for evil behavior. However, it can take root in people whose cravings for evil behavior have been dispelled by the Lord. In these the seed can take root—that is, the truth can take root in their spiritual minds (see the close of §86 above).

91. It is generally thought nowadays that being saved is a matter of believing one thing or another that the church teaches, and that being saved is not a matter of obeying the Ten Commandments in particular—not killing, not committing adultery, not stealing, not bearing false witness; and it is said in a wider sense that the focus should not be on deeds but on faith that comes from God. However, to the extent that we are caught up in evils we do not have faith (see *Life* 42–52). Consult your reason and you will clearly see that no killer, adulterer, thief, or false witness can have faith while he or she is caught up in such cravings. You will also clearly see that we cannot dispel these cravings in any other way than by our being unwilling to act on them because they are sins—that is, because they are hellish and diabolical. So if people think that being saved is a matter of believing one thing or another that the church teaches, while at the same time they remain people of this kind, they cannot help being foolish. This is according to what the Lord says in Matthew 7:26.

This is how Jeremiah describes this kind of church:

Stand in the gate of the house of Jehovah and proclaim this word there: "Thus says Jehovah Sabaoth, the God of Israel: 'Make your ways and your deeds good. Do not put your trust in lying words, saying, "The temple of Jehovah, the temple of Jehovah, the temple of Jehovah are these." Are you going to steal, kill, commit adultery, and tell lies under oath, and then come and stand before me in this house that bears my name and say, "We are delivered" when you are doing these abominations? Has this house become a robbers' cave? Indeed, behold, I have seen it,' says Jehovah." (Jeremiah 7:2, 3, 4, 9, 10, 11)

The Only Way to Abstain from Sinful Evils So Thoroughly That We Develop an Inner Aversion to Them Is to Do Battle against Them

92. Everyone knows on the basis of the Word and teachings drawn from it that from the time we are born our self-centeredness is evil and that this is why we have an inborn compulsion to love evil behavior and to be drawn into it. We are deliberately vengeful, for example; we deliberately cheat, disparage others, and commit adultery; and if we do not think that these behaviors are sins and resist them for that reason, we do them whenever the opportunity presents itself, as long as our reputation or our wealth is not affected.

Then too, we really enjoy doing such things if we have no religion.

93. Since this self-centeredness is the taproot of the life we lead, we can see what kind of trees we would be if this root were not pulled up and a new root planted. We would be rotten trees that needed to be cut down and thrown into the fire (see Matthew 3:10; 7:19).

This root is not removed and a new one put in its place unless we see that the evils that constitute it are harmful to our souls, and therefore we want to banish them. However, since they are part of our self-centeredness and therefore give us pleasure, we can do this only reluctantly and in the face of opposition, and therefore by doing battle.

94. Everyone undertakes this battle who believes that heaven and hell are real and that heaven is eternal happiness and hell eternal misery, and who believes that we come into hell if we do evil and into heaven if we do good. Whenever we do battle in this way, we are acting from our inner selves and against the compulsions that constitute the root of evil, because when we are fighting against something we are not intending it, and compulsions are intentions.

We can see from this that the only way to dig out the root of evil is by doing battle against it.

95. The more we do battle and thereby set evils to one side, the more what is good replaces them and we look what is evil in the face from the perspective of what is good and see that the evil is hellish and hideous. Since this is how we see it then, we not only abstain from it but develop an aversion to it and eventually loathe it.

96. When we battle against what is evil, we cannot help but fight using what seems to be our own strength, because if we are not using what seems to be our own strength, we are not doing battle. We are standing there like an automaton, seeing nothing and doing nothing, while constantly thinking on the basis of evil and in favor of it, not against it.

However, we need to be quite clear about the fact that it is the Lord alone who is fighting within us against the evils, that it only seems as though we are using our own strength for the battle, and that the Lord wants it to seem like that because if it does not, no battle occurs, so there is no reformation either.

97. This battle is hard only if we have given free rein to our cravings and indulged in them deliberately, or if we have stubbornly rejected the holy principles of the Word and the church. Otherwise, it is not hard. We need only resist evils in our intentions once a week or twice a month and we will notice a change.

98. The Christian church is called "the church militant." It is called that because it fights against the Devil and therefore against evils that come from hell. (*The Devil* is hell.) The inner trials that church people endure are that fight.

99. There are many passages in the Word about battles against evils, or trials. That is what these words of the Lord are about:

> I say to you, unless a grain of wheat falls into the ground and dies, it remains alone; but if it dies, it produces much fruit. (John 12:24)

Then there is this:

> Those who wish to come with me must deny themselves and take up their cross and follow me. Those who try to save their own life will lose it, but those who lose their life for my sake and the gospel's will save it. (Mark 8:34, 35)

The *cross* means these trials, as it does also in Matthew 10:38; 16:24; Mark 10:21; and Luke 14:27. *Life* means the life we claim as our own, as it does also in Matthew 10:39; 16:25; Luke 9:24; and especially John 12:25. It is also the life of "the flesh," which "is of no benefit at all" (John 6:63). In the book of Revelation, the Lord spoke to all the churches about battles against evils and victories over them:

> To *the church in Ephesus:* To those who overcome I will give [food] to eat from the tree of life, which is in the midst of the paradise of God. (Revelation 2:7)

> To *the church in Smyrna:* Those who overcome will not be hurt by the second death. (Revelation 2:11)

> To *the church in Pergamum:* To those who overcome I will give the hidden manna to eat; and I will give them a white stone, and on the stone a new name written that no one knows except the one who receives it. (Revelation 2:17)

> To *the church in Thyatira:* To those who overcome and keep my works to the end I will give power over the nations, and give the morning star. (Revelation 2:26, 28)

To *the church in Sardis:* [Those who overcome will be clothed in white garments, and I will not blot their names from the Book of Life; I will confess their names before my Father and before his angels. (Revelation 3:5)

To *the church in Philadelphia:*] Those who overcome I will make pillars in the temple of my God, and will write upon them the name of God, the name of the city of God, the New Jerusalem, which is coming down out of heaven from God, and my new name. (Revelation 3:12)

To *the church in Laodicea:* To those who overcome I will grant to sit with me on my throne. (Revelation 3:21) . . .

We Need to Abstain from Sinful Evils and Fight against Them As Though We Were Doing So on Our Own

101. It is part of the divine design that we act in freedom and according to reason, because acting in freedom according to reason is acting on our own.

However, these two powers, freedom and reason, are not our own. They are the Lord's within us; and since we are human they are not taken from us, because we cannot be reformed without them. That is, we cannot practice repentance, we cannot fight against evils and as a result bear fruit that is consistent with repentance [Matthew 3:8; Luke 3:8].

So since we are given freedom and reason by the Lord and we act from them, it follows that we are not acting on our own but as though we were on our own.

102. The Lord loves us and wants to dwell with us but cannot love and dwell with us unless he is received and loved in return. This is the one and only means to union. This is why the Lord gives us freedom and the power to reason—the freedom of thinking and intending with seeming autonomy, and the power of reason that serves as our guide. It is impossible to love and be united with someone who is unresponsive, impossible to come in and abide with someone who is unreceptive. It is because our own receptiveness and responsiveness are given by the Lord that the Lord said,

Abide in me, and I [will abide] in you. (John 15:4)

Those who abide in me and in whom I abide bear much fruit. (John 15:5)

On that day you will know that you are in me and I am in you. (John 14:20)

The Lord also tells us that he is present in whatever is true and good that we have received and that is within us:

If you abide in me and my words abide in you . . . If you keep my commandments, you will abide in my love. (John 15:7, 10)

The people who love me are those who have my commandments and do them; and I will love them and dwell with them. (John 14:21, 23)

So the Lord dwells with us in what is his own, and we dwell in what the Lord is giving us and are therefore in the Lord.

103. Since the Lord gives us this ability to respond in turn—and therefore a mutual relationship [with him]—he says that we are to repent, and no one can repent without a sense of autonomy.

Jesus said, "Unless you repent, you will all perish." (Luke 13:3, 5)

Jesus said, "The kingdom of God is at hand. Repent, and believe in the gospel." (Mark 1:14, 15)

Jesus said, "I have come to call sinners to repentance." (Luke 5:32)

Jesus said to the churches, "Repent!" (Revelation 2:5, 16, 21, 22; 3:3)

They did not repent of their deeds. (Revelation 16:11)

104. Since the Lord gives us this ability to respond in turn—and therefore a mutual relationship [with him]—the Lord says that we are to do his commandments and bear fruit:

Why do you call me, "Lord, Lord," and not do what I say? (Luke 6:46–49)

If you know these things, you are blessed if you do them. (John 13:17)

You are my friends if you do what I command you. (John 15:14)

Whoever does and teaches [the commandments] will be called great in the kingdom of the heavens. (Matthew 5:19)

Everyone who hears my words and does them I will liken to a wise man. (Matthew 7:24)

Bear fruit that is consistent with repentance. (Matthew 3:8)

Make the tree good and its fruit good. (Matthew 12:33)

The kingdom will be given to a nation that bears its fruits. (Matthew 21:43)

Every tree that does not bear fruit is cut down and thrown into the fire. (Matthew 7:19)

We can see from these passages that we are to act [not] on our own, but through the power of the Lord, which we must pray for; and that this is acting as if we were on our own.

105. Since the Lord gives us this ability to respond in turn—and therefore a mutual relationship [with him]—we must therefore give an account of our deeds and be recompensed accordingly, for the Lord says:

The Son of Humanity is going to come, and he will repay all people according to their deeds. (Matthew 16:27)

Those who have done what is good will go forth into the resurrection of life, and those who have done what is evil will go forth into the resurrection of condemnation. (John 5:29)

Their works follow them. (Revelation 14:13)

All were judged according to their works. (Revelation 20:13)

Behold, I am coming, and my reward is with me, to give to all according to what they have done. (Revelation 22:12)

If we had no ability to respond, we could not be held accountable.

106. Since it is up to us to be receptive and to respond in turn, the church teaches that we are to examine ourselves, confess our sins in the presence of God, stop committing them, and lead a new life. Every church in the Christian world teaches this, as stated in *Life* 3–8.

107. If we did not have the power to be receptive and therefore had no apparent ability to think independently, faith could not have even entered the discussion, since faith does not come from us either. If it were not for that ability to be receptive, we would be like straw blowing in the wind, and would stand around lifelessly, with our mouths gaping and our hands hanging limp, waiting for something to flow in, neither thinking nor doing anything about what matters for our salvation. We are in no way the active force in these matters, true, but we do react seemingly on our own.

These matters will be presented in still clearer light, though, in the works on angelic wisdom.

If We Turn Our Backs on Evils for Any Other Reason Than That They Are Sins, We Are Not Turning Our Backs on Them but Are Simply Making Sure They Are Not Visible in the Eyes of the World

108. There are moral individuals who keep the commandments of the second tablet of the Ten Commandments, who do not cheat, blaspheme, take vengeance, or commit adultery, and who are convinced that such behavior is evil because it

is harmful to the state and therefore contrary to the laws of humanity. They also practice goodwill, honesty, fairness, and chastity.

If they are doing these good things and turning their backs on evil things only because the latter are evil, though, and not because they are sins as well, these people are merely earthly, and in merely earthly individuals the root of the evil remains in place and is not removed. So the good things they do are not good, because they arise from the doers themselves.

109. Moral earthly individuals can look just like moral spiritual individuals to people on earth, but not to angels in heaven. To angels in heaven they look like lifeless wooden statues if the individuals are focused on goodness, and like lifeless marble statues if they are focused on truth. It is different for moral spiritual individuals because a moral earthly person is moral on the outside, while a moral spiritual person is moral on the inside, and the outside has no life apart from the inside. Technically speaking, the outside is alive, of course, but it has no life worthy of the name.

110. The compulsions to evil that constitute our deeper nature from birth can be set aside only by the Lord, because the Lord flows from what is spiritual into what is earthly, but of ourselves we flow from what is earthly into what is spiritual. This latter flow goes against the divine design and does not operate on our compulsions and set them aside but envelops them more and more tightly as we reinforce them. So since this means that our inherited evil remains hidden and enclosed within us, when we become spirits after death it bursts the coverings that veiled it on earth and breaks out like pus from an ulcer that has been healed only superficially.

111. The reasons we may be moral in outward form are many and varied, but if we are not inwardly moral as well, we are not really moral at all. For example, we may refrain from adultery and fornication out of fear of civil law and its penalties, fear of loss of our good name and therefore our rank, fear of associated diseases, fear of being berated by a wife at home and a consequent loss of tranquility, fear of vengeance by a husband or relatives. We may refrain because of poverty or greed, because of incompetence caused by disease, abuse, age, or impotence—in fact, if we refrain from them because of any earthly or moral law and not because of spiritual law as well, we are adulterers and lechers all the same. That is, we believe that they are not sins and in our spirits regard them as not illegal in the sight of God. This means that in spirit we are committing them even though we are not doing so in the flesh in this world; so when we become spirits after death, we speak openly in favor of them.

We can see from this that irreligious people can turn their backs on evils as harmful, but only Christians can turn their backs on evils because they are sins.

112. It is much the same with all kinds of theft and cheating, all kinds of killing and vengeance, all kinds of false witness and lying. None of us can be cleansed and purified from them by our own strength. There are infinite complexities hidden within a compulsion that we see as a single, simple thing, but the Lord sees the tiniest details in complete sequence.

In a word, we cannot regenerate ourselves. That is, we cannot form a new heart and a new spirit within ourselves [Ezekiel 11:19; 36:26]. Only the Lord, who is the true Reformer and Regenerator, can do this; so if we try to make ourselves new with our own plans and our own intelligence, this is like putting rouge on a disfigured face or smearing cleansing cream over an area that is inwardly infected.

113. That is why the Lord says in Matthew,

Blind Pharisee, cleanse the inside of the cup and the plate first, so that the outside of them may be clean as well. (Matthew 23:26) and in Isaiah,

> Wash yourselves! Purify yourselves! Take away the evil of your deeds from *before my eyes!* Stop doing evil! And then, even if your sins have been like scarlet, they will become white like snow; even if they have been as red as purple-dyed cloth, they will be like wool. (Isaiah 1:16, 18)

True Christianity (1771)

The Catechism, or Ten Commandments, Explained in Both Its Outer and Its Inner Meanings

282. Every nation on the face of the earth knows that it is evil to murder, to commit adultery, to steal, and to bear false witness, and knows that any country, state, or civilized society that did not forbid these evils would be doomed. No one thinks the Israelite nation was stupider than other nations and did not know these things were evils. Anyone might be amazed, then, that these laws, universally recognized on earth as they are, were delivered on Mount Sinai in such a miraculous way by Jehovah himself.

I have been told, though, that they were delivered in this miraculous way so that people would know that these laws are not only civil and moral laws but divine laws as well. Therefore to act against them would be not only doing something evil to our neighbor (meaning our fellow citizen and our community) but also sinning against God. When they were delivered by Jehovah on Mount Sinai, therefore, these laws became laws of religion as well. It should be obvious that whatever Jehovah commands, he commands as an aspect of religion; therefore his commands are something we need to follow for the sake of our salvation. Before I explain the Commandments, though, I will give a prefatory statement about their holiness, to show that they have religious import.

The Ten Commandments Were the Holiest Thing in the Israelite Church

283. The Ten Commandments are the most important thing in the Word. As a result, they were the most important thing in the church that was established in the Israelite nation. In a brief encapsulation they included all the elements of religion that provide for God's connection to us and our connection to God. Therefore the Ten Commandments were the holiest thing of all.

The following points show that the Ten Commandments were the holiest thing: Jehovah the Lord himself, together with angels, came down on Mount Sinai in fire and delivered the Ten Commandments by direct speech. The mountain was fenced all around so that no one would approach and die. Not even the priests or the elders were allowed to approach; only Moses. The commandments were written on two tablets of stone by the finger of God. When Moses carried the tablets down for the second time, his face was glowing.

Afterward, the tablets were stored in an ark that was at the heart of the tabernacle. There was a mercy seat on top of the ark with angel guardians made of gold over it. The inmost area in the tabernacle, where the ark was placed, was called the most holy place. Outside the veil behind which the ark stood there were several things that represented holy things in heaven and the church: a table overlaid with gold that had the showbread on it, a golden altar for burning incense, and a golden lampstand with seven lamps. There was also a curtain around the tabernacle made out of [threads of] fine linen and of purple and scarlet [yarn]. The holiness of the whole tabernacle came from no other source than the law that was inside the ark.

Because of the holiness of the tabernacle that came from the law in the ark, the entire Israelite population camped around the tabernacle, tribe by tribe, in an arrangement that was given by command. When they traveled, the tribes moved in a specific sequence behind the ark, and there was a cloud over the ark by day and a fire by night.

Because of the holiness of this law and Jehovah's presence in it, Jehovah spoke to Moses from over the mercy seat between the angel guardians. In fact, the ark was called "Jehovah" there. Aaron was not allowed inside the veil unless he offered sacrifices and burned incense, or else he would die.

Because of Jehovah's presence in this law and surrounding it, the ark containing the law performed miracles. For example, the waters of the Jordan were split apart, and as long as the ark was resting in the middle of the riverbed the people crossed on dry land. When the ark was carried around the walls of Jericho, the walls fell. Dagon, an idol of the Philistines, at first fell facedown before the ark. Later, Dagon lay decapitated with the palms of its hands across the threshold of the shrine. Because of the ark, as many as several thousand inhabitants of Beth-shemesh were struck down. Uzza died because he touched the ark. David brought the ark back into Zion with sacrifices and shouts of triumph. Later on Solomon brought the ark into the Temple in Jerusalem where he had made a sanctuary for it; and so on. All these things make it clear that the Ten Commandments were the holiest thing in the Israelite church. . . .

285. Since this law provides for the Lord's partnership with us and our partnership with the Lord, it is called *the covenant* and *the testimony*. It is called the covenant because it provides for partnership; it is called the testimony because it confirms the agreements in the covenant. In the Word a *covenant* means a partnership and *testimony* means something confirming and witnessing to its agreements. This is why there were two tablets, one for God and one for us. The partnership comes from the Lord, but it comes when we do the things that have been written on our tablet. The Lord is constantly present and wanting to come in, but we have to use the freedom we have been given by the Lord to open the door. He says, "Behold! I am standing at the door and knocking. If any hear my voice and open the door, I will come in and will dine with them and they with me" (Revelation 3:20).

The stone tablets on which the law was engraved were called *the tablets of the covenant*. Because of them the ark was called *the ark of the covenant* and the law itself was called *the covenant* (see Numbers 10:33; Deuteronomy 4:13, 23; 5:2, 3; 9:9; Joshua 3:11; 1 Kings 8:21; Revelation 11:19; and elsewhere).

Because *covenant* means partnership, it is said of the Lord that he will be *a covenant for the people* (Isaiah 42:6; 49:9). He is also called the angel or messenger of the covenant (Malachi 3:1), and his blood is called the blood of the covenant (Matthew 26:28; Zechariah 9:11; Exodus 24:4–10). This is why the Word is called the Old Covenant and the New Covenant. Covenants are made for love, friendship, association, and partnership.

286. There was tremendous holiness and power in this law because it is a synopsis of all the elements of religion. It was engraved on two tablets, one of which contains a synopsis of all things related to God, and the other, a synopsis of all things related to us. For this reason the commandments of this law are called the *Ten Words* (Exodus 34:28; Deuteronomy 4:13; 10:4). They are called this because *ten* means all and *words* mean truths. Of course, they contained more than ten words. For an explanation that *ten* means all, and that tithes were established because of that meaning, see *Revelation Unveiled*

101; on the point that this law is a synopsis of all aspects of religion, see below [§289].

In Their Literal Meaning, the Ten Commandments Contain General Principles to Be Taught and Lived; in Their Spiritual and Heavenly Meanings, They Contain Absolutely Everything

287. It is generally recognized that the Ten Commandments in the Word are called the law in a supreme sense because they contain all the principles to be taught and lived. They contain not only all the principles related to God but also all the principles related to us. For this reason this law was engraved on two tablets, one of which relates to God and the other to us.

It is also generally recognized that all the principles to be taught and lived come down to loving God and loving our neighbor. The Ten Commandments contain all the teachings about these two kinds of love. The entire Word teaches nothing else, as the Lord's words make clear:

> Jesus said, "You are to love the Lord your God with all your heart, with all your soul, and with all your mind; and your neighbor as yourself. The Law and the Prophets hinge on these two commandments." (Matthew 22:37–40)

The Law and the Prophets means the entire Word.

Further,

> A lawyer tested Jesus by saying, "Master, what should I do to inherit eternal life?" Jesus said to him, "What has been written in the law? How do you read it?" He replied, "You are to love the Lord your God with all your heart, with all your soul, with all your strength, and with all your mind, and your neighbor as yourself." And Jesus said, "Do this and you will live." (Luke 10:25–28)

Because everything in the Word is about loving God and loving our neighbor, and the first tablet of the Ten Commandments contains a summary of everything about loving God while the second tablet contains a summary of everything about loving our neighbor, it follows that the Ten Commandments contain everything to be taught and lived.

If you visualize the two tablets, it is clear how they are connected. God looks at us from his tablet and we look at God from ours. The two tablets are therefore turned toward each other. On God's side it never fails that he is looking at us and doing what has to be done for our salvation. If we accept and do the things on our tablet, a reciprocal partnership [with God] develops. What happens to us then is indicated by the Lord's words to the lawyer: "Do this and you will live."

288. The Word often mentions *the law*. I will now say what that means in a narrow sense, in a broader sense, and in the broadest sense. In a narrow sense, *the law* means the Ten Commandments. In a broader sense, *the law* means the rules that Moses gave to the children of Israel. In the broadest sense, *the law* means the entire Word.

People know that *in a narrow sense "the law" means the Ten Commandments.*

In a broader sense, "the law" means the rules that Moses gave to the children of Israel. This becomes clear from the individual rules laid out in Exodus—they are called *the law*:

This is the law of the trespass offering. (Leviticus 7:1)

This is the law of the sacrifice of peace offerings. (Leviticus 7:11)

This is the law of the grain offering. (Leviticus 6:14 and following)

This is the law of the burnt offering, the grain offering, the sacrifices for sin and guilt, and the consecrations. (Leviticus 7:37)

This is the law of the animals and the birds. (Leviticus 11:46 and following)

This is the law for a woman who has given birth to a son or a daughter. (Leviticus 12:7)

This is the law of leprosy. (Leviticus 13:59; 14:2, 32, 54, 57)

This is the law for someone who has a discharge. (Leviticus 15:32)

This is the law of jealousy. (Numbers 5:29, 30)

This is the law of the Nazirite. (Numbers 6:13, 21)

This is the law of cleansing. (Numbers 19:14)

This is the law of the red heifer. (Numbers 19:2)

[This is] the law for a king. (Deuteronomy 17:15–19)

In fact, the entire five books of Moses are called "the Law" (Deuteronomy 31:9, 11, 12, 26). They are called this in the New Testament as well (Luke 2:22; 24:44; John 1:45; 7:22, 23; 8:5; and elsewhere).

When Paul says, "We are justified by faith apart from the works of the Law" (Romans 3:28), by *the works of the Law* he means the rules just mentioned. This is clear from the words that follow this passage in Romans, as well as from Paul's words to Peter chiding him for making others follow Jewish religious practices. In the latter context, Paul says three times in one verse, "No one is justified by the works of the Law" (Galatians 2:14, 16).

In the broadest sense, "the law" means the entire Word. This is clear from the following passages: "Jesus said, 'Is it not written *in your law*, "You are gods"?'" (John 10:34, referring to something written in Psalms 82:6). "The crowd answered, 'We have heard from *the law* that Christ remains forever'"

(John 12:34, referring to something written in Psalms 89:29; 110:4; and Daniel 7:14). "This was to fulfill the Word that was written in *their law*, 'They hated me for no reason'" (John 15:25, referring to something written in Psalms 35:19). "The Pharisees said, 'Do any of the rulers believe in him? But the crowd does, who do not know *the law*'" (John 7:48, 49). "It is easier for heaven and earth to pass away than for *the tip of one letter of the law* to fall" (Luke 16:17). In these passages, *the law* means the entire Sacred Scripture. There are a thousand passages like this in [the Psalms of] David.

289. In their spiritual and heavenly meanings, the Ten Commandments contain absolutely all the instructions to be taught and lived—all aspects of faith and goodwill. This is because each and every thing on both a large and a small scale in the Word's literal meaning conceals two inner meanings. One inner meaning is called spiritual, and the other, heavenly. Divine truth exists in its own light and divine goodness exists in its own warmth within these meanings. Because the Word has these characteristics as a whole and in each of its parts, the Ten Commandments need to be explained in all three meanings, called the earthly meaning, the spiritual meaning, and the heavenly meaning.

290. If people were not told what the Word is like, none of them could have any idea that there is an infinity in the Word's least details, meaning that it contains things beyond number that not even the angels could ever fully draw out. Everything in it is comparable to a seed that has the capability of growing out of the ground to become a huge tree, which produces a tremendous number of seeds that are capable in turn of producing similar trees that together make up a whole grove, whose seeds in turn lead to many groves, and so on to infinity. This is the nature of the Lord's Word on a detailed level; it is especially true of the Ten Commandments. Because they teach love for God and love for our neighbor, they are a brief synopsis of the entire Word.

In fact, the Lord used a similar analogy to explain that this is the nature of the Word:

> The kingdom of God is like a grain of mustard seed that someone took and sowed in a field. It is the least of all seeds, but when it has grown, it is bigger than all other plants and becomes a tree so that the birds of the air come and nest in its branches. (Matthew 13:31, 32; Mark 4:31, 32; Luke 13:18, 19; compare also Ezekiel 17:2–8)

If you think about angelic wisdom, you can see that the Word has this infinity of spiritual seeds, or truths. All angelic wisdom comes from the Word and grows inside the angels to eternity. The wiser they become, the more clearly they see that wisdom has no end, and the more clearly they perceive that they themselves are only in its front hall; they could never in the least touch the Lord's divine wisdom, which they call a bottomless depth. Since the Word comes from this bottomless depth, in that it is from the Lord, clearly all its parts have a kind of infinity.

The First Commandment
There Is to Be No Other God before My Face

291. These are the words of the first commandment (Exodus 20:3; Deuteronomy 5:7). In their *earthly meaning*, which is their literal meaning, the most accessible sense is that we must not worship idols; for it goes on to say,

> You are not to make yourself a sculpture or any form that is in the heavens above or the earth below or in the waters under the earth. You are not to bow yourself down to them, and you are not to worship them, because *I, Jehovah your God, am a jealous God.* (Exodus 20:4, 5)

The most accessible meaning of this commandment is that we must not worship idols, because before the time [when this commandment was given] and after it right up to the coming of the Lord much of the Middle East had idolatrous worship. What caused the idolatrous worship was that all the churches before the Lord came were symbolic and emblematic. Their symbols and emblems were designed to present divine attributes in different forms and sculpted shapes. When the meanings of these forms were lost, common people began worshipping the forms as gods.

The Israelite nation had this kind of worship in Egypt, as you can see from the golden calf that they worshipped in the wilderness instead of worshipping Jehovah. That type of worship never became foreign to them, as you can see from many passages in both the historical and the prophetical parts of the Word.

292. This commandment, *There is to be no other God before my face*, also has an earthly meaning that we must not worship any person, dead or alive, as a god. Worshipping people as gods was another practice in the Middle East and in various surrounding areas. The many gods of the nations there were of this type, such as Baal, Ashtoreth, Chemosh, Milcom, and Beelzebub. In Athens and Rome there were Saturn, Jupiter, Neptune, Pluto, Apollo, Athena, and so on. People worshipped some of these at first as holy people, then as supernatural beings, and finally as gods. The fact that these nations also worshipped living people as gods can be seen from the edict of Darius the Mede that for a thirty-day period no one was to ask anything of God, only of the king, or be thrown into the lions' den (Daniel 6:8–28).

293. In the earthly meaning, which is the literal meaning, the first commandment also entails that we are to love above all else no one except God and nothing except what comes

from God. This also accords with the Lord's words (Matthew 22:37–39; Luke 10:25–28). Someone we love above all else is a god to us; and something we love above all else is divine to us. For example, if we love ourselves above all else, or if we love the world above all else, to us we ourselves are our god, or else the world is. This explains why under these circumstances we do not believe at heart in any god; because of this we are connected to people like ourselves in hell, where all are gathered who have loved themselves or the world above all else.

294. The *spiritual meaning* of this commandment is that we must worship no other God except the Lord Jesus Christ, because he is Jehovah, and he came into the world and brought about redemption. If he had not done so, not one person and not one angel could have been saved.

It is clear from the following passages in the Word that there is no other God except him:

> It will be said in that day, "Behold, this is our God. We have waited for him to free us. This is Jehovah whom we have waited for. Let us rejoice and be glad in his salvation." (Isaiah 25:9)

> The voice of one crying in the desert, "Prepare a way for Jehovah; make a level pathway in the solitude for our God. For the glory of Jehovah will be revealed, and all flesh will see it together. Behold, the Lord Jehovih is coming with strength; like a shepherd he will feed his flock." (Isaiah 40:3, 5, 11)

> "The only God is among you; there is no other God." Surely you are the God who was hidden, O God *the Savior* of Israel. (Isaiah 45:14, 15)

. . . These passages make it very clear that the Lord our Savior is Jehovah himself, who is the Creator, the Redeemer, and the Regenerator in one. This is the spiritual meaning of this commandment.

295. The *heavenly meaning of this commandment* is that the Lord Jehovah is infinite, immeasurable, and eternal; and omnipotent, omniscient, and omnipresent. He is the First and the Last; the Beginning and the End; the One who was, is, and will be. He is love itself and wisdom itself, or goodness itself and truth itself. Therefore he is life itself. He is the sole being; all things come from him.

296. All people who acknowledge and worship another god besides the Lord the Savior Jesus Christ, who is Jehovah God himself in human form, sin against this first commandment. So do all those who convince themselves that there are three actually existing divine persons from eternity. As these people reinforce themselves in this mistake, they become more and more earthly and mindless. They cannot inwardly comprehend any divine truth. If they hear and accept divine truth, they nonetheless pollute it and wrap it in mistaken ideas. For this reason they can be compared to people who live on the lowest or underground level of a house—they do not hear any of the conversation of people on the second or third floors, because the ceiling over their heads stops the sound from getting through.

[2] The human mind is like a three-story house that contains people on the bottom floor who have convinced themselves that there have been three gods from eternity, while on the second and third floors there are people who acknowledge and believe in one God in a human form that can be seen—the Lord God the Savior.

People who are mindlessly physical and utterly earthly are actually complete animals; the only thing that differentiates them from true brute animals is their ability to speak and to make false inferences. They are like someone who lives at a zoo where there are wild animals of every kind, who plays the lion one day, the bear the next, the tiger the next, the leopard or the wolf the next, and could play a sheep but would be laughing inside.

[3] People who are merely earthly think about divine truths only on the basis of worldly phenomena and the mistaken impressions of their own senses. They cannot lift their minds above them. As a result, their body of religious teaching could be compared to a soup made of chaff that they eat as if it were the finest cuisine. Or their body of teaching could be compared to the loaf of bread and the cakes that Ezekiel the prophet was commanded to mix from wheat, barley, beans, lentils, spelt, and human excrement or cow dung in order to represent what the church was like in the Israelite nation (Ezekiel 4:9 and following). It is the same with the body of teaching of a church that is founded and built on the idea of three divine persons from eternity, each of whom is individually god.

[4] By picturing it mentally as it truly is, anyone can see the hideous wrongness of this faith. It is like three people standing next to each other in a row: the first person is distinguished by a crown and a scepter; the second person's right hand is holding a book, which is the Word, while his left hand holds a golden cross spattered in blood; and the third person has wings strapped on and stands on one foot in an effort to fly off and take action. Over the three there is an inscription: *These three people, each of whom is a god, are one God.* Any wise man would see this picture and say to himself, "That's ridiculously unrealistic!"

He would say something very different if he saw a picture of one divine person whose head was surrounded with rays of heavenly light, with the inscription: *This is our God—our Creator, Redeemer, and Regenerator in one, and therefore our Savior.* He would kiss this picture and take it home next to his heart, and when he and his wife and their children and servants would look at it they would feel uplifted.

The Second Commandment

*You Are Not to Take the Name of Jehovah Your
God in Vain, Because Jehovah Will Not Hold
Guiltless Someone Who Takes His Name in Vain*

297. In its *earthly meaning*, which is the literal meaning, taking the name of Jehovah God in vain includes abusing his name in various types of talking, especially in lies and deceptions, in swearing and oath-taking for no reason or to avoid blame; and using his name with evil intent, which is cursing, or in sorcery and magic spells.

To swear by God or by his holiness, by the Word or by the Gospel during coronations, inaugurations into the priesthood, and confirmations of faith is not taking God's name in vain, unless the people who take the oath later reject their promises as impossible or pointless.

Furthermore, because it is holiness itself, the name of God is used constantly in the sacred activities of the church, such as in prayers, hymns, and all aspects of worship, as well as in sermons and books on church-related topics. The reason is that God is in every aspect of religion. When he is ritually called forth by his name, he is present and hears. In these activities the name of God is kept holy.

The name of Jehovah God is intrinsically holy, as you can see by the fact that after their earliest times the Jews did not dare, nor do they now dare, to say the name Jehovah. Out of respect for the Jews, the Gospel writers and apostles did not want to say the name either. Instead of *Jehovah* they said *the Lord*, as you can see from passages from the Old Testament that are quoted in the New Testament but use *the Lord* instead of *Jehovah*, such as Matthew 22:37 and Luke 10:27 that quote Deuteronomy 6:5, and so on.

The name of Jesus is also holy, as people generally know because the apostle said that at that name knees bend and should bend in heaven and on earth [Philippians 2:10]. For another thing, no devil in hell can pronounce the name Jesus.

There are many names for God that are not to be taken in vain: Jehovah, Jehovah God, Jehovah Sabaoth, the Holy One of Israel, Jesus, Christ, and the Holy Spirit.

298. In the *spiritual meaning*, the name of God stands for everything that the church teaches on the basis of the Word— everything through which the Lord is called on and worshipped. Taken together, all these are names for God. Taking God's name in vain, then, means misusing any of these things for idle chatter, lies, deceptions, curses, sorcery, or magic spells. This too is abusing and blaspheming God, and therefore his name.

From the following passages you can see that the Word and anything from it that is used in the church or in any worship is God's name:

> From the rising of the sun my name will be invoked. (Isaiah 41:25)

> From the rising of the sun to the setting of it, great is my name among the nations. In every place incense is offered to my name. But you desecrate my name when you say, "Jehovah's table is defiled." And you sneeze at my name when you bring offerings that are stolen, lame, and sick. (Malachi 1:11, 12, 13)

> All peoples walk in the name of their God; we walk in the name of Jehovah our God. (Micah 4:5)

> They are to worship Jehovah in one place, the place where he will put his name (Deuteronomy 12:5, 11, 13, 14, 18; 16:2, 6, 11, 15, 16),

that is, where Jehovah will locate their worship of him.

> Jesus said, "Where two or three are gathered together in my name, I am there in the midst of them." (Matthew 18:20)

As many as received him, he gave them power to be children of God, if they believed in his name. (John 1:12)

Those who do not believe have already been judged because they have not believed in the name of the only begotten Son of God. (John 3:18)

Those who believe will have life in his name. (John 20:31)

Jesus said, "I have revealed your name to people and have made your name known to them." (John 17:26)

The Lord said, "You have a few names in Sardis." (Revelation 3:4)

There are also many passages similar to these in which the name of God means the divine quality which radiates from God and through which he is worshipped.

The name of Jesus Christ, however, means everything related to his redeeming humankind and everything related to his teaching, and therefore everything through which he saves. *Jesus* means all his efforts to save the human race through redemption; *Christ* means all his efforts to save the human race through teaching.

299. In the *heavenly meaning*, taking the Lord's name in vain parallels what the Lord said to the Pharisees:

All sin and blasphemy is forgiven people, but blasphemy of the Spirit is not forgiven. (Matthew 12:31, 32)

Blasphemy of the Spirit means blasphemy against the divinity of the Lord's human manifestation and against the holiness of the Word.

In the highest or heavenly meaning, the *name of Jehovah God* stands for the Lord's divine-human manifestation, as the following passages make clear:

Jesus said, *"Father, glorify your name."* And a voice came out of heaven that said, "I both have glorified it and will glorify it again." (John 12:27, 28)

Whatever you ask in my name, I will do it, so that the Father is glorified in the Son. If you ask anything in my name, I will do it. (John 14:13, 14)

In the heavenly sense the phrase in the Lord's prayer "Your name must be kept holy" [Matthew 6:9] has the same meaning, as does the word "name" in Exodus 23:21 and Isaiah 63:16.

Since Matthew 12:31 and 32 says that "blasphemy of the Spirit" is not forgiven us, and this is what the heavenly meaning refers to, for this reason the following phrase is added to this commandment: *because Jehovah will not hold guiltless someone who takes his name in vain.*

300. The nature of names in the spiritual world makes it clear that someone's *name* does not mean her or his name alone but also her or his full nature. In that world, people all stop using the names they were given in baptism in this world and the names they received from their parents or their family. All there are named for what they are like. Angels get a name that indicates the moral and spiritual life they have. In fact, the Lord was referring to angels in the following passage:

Jesus said, "I am the good shepherd. The sheep hear the shepherd's voice and he calls his sheep by name and leads them out." (John 10:3, 11)

The same holds true in the following passage:

I have a few names in Sardis who have not defiled their clothes. Upon the person who conquers I will write the name of the city New Jerusalem and my new name. (Revelation 3:4, 12)

Gabriel and *Michael* are not the names of two people in heaven—these names mean all the angels in heaven who have wisdom about the Lord and who worship him. The names of people and places in the Word do not mean people and places either; they mean aspects of the church.

Even in our world a *name* means more than just a name—it also means what someone is like. People's natures get attached to their names. We often say, "They're doing it for their name" or "to make a name for themselves." "Those are big names" means that those people are famous for characteristics they possess, such as creativity, scholarship, achievements, or the like.

It is common knowledge that people who insult or libel other people's names are in fact insulting or libeling the actions of the other people's lives. The two are conceptually linked. Such attacks ruin the reputation of people's names. Likewise, someone who says the name of a monarch, a duke, or a great person with disrespect also dishonors the person's majesty and dignity. It is equally true that someone who mentions anyone's name with a tone of contempt also disparages the deeds of that person's life—this applies to everyone. Every country has laws that forbid us to abuse, attack, or insult anyone's name (meaning anyone's nature and reputation).

The Third Commandment
Remember the Sabbath Day in Order to Keep It Holy; for Six Days You Will Labor and Do All Your Work, but the Seventh Day Is the Sabbath for Jehovah Your God

301. This is the third commandment, as you can see in Exodus 20:8, 9, 10; and Deuteronomy 5:12, 13, 14. In the *earthly meaning*, which is the literal meaning, it indicates that there are six days that belong to us and our labors, and a seventh day that belongs to the Lord and to the peaceful rest that he gives us. In the original language *Sabbath* means rest.

The Sabbath was the holiest thing among the children of Israel because it represented the Lord. The six days represented his labors and battles with the hells. The seventh day represented his victory over the hells and the resulting rest. That day was holiness itself because it represented the completion of the Lord's entire redemption.

When the Lord came into the world, however, and therefore symbols representing him were no longer needed, the Sabbath day was turned into a day for instruction in divine things, for rest from labors, for meditating on things related to salvation and eternal life, and for loving our neighbor.

It is clear that the Sabbath became a day for instruction in divine things, because the Lord taught on the Sabbath day in the Temple and in synagogues (Mark 6:2; Luke 4:16, 31, 32; 13:10). On the Sabbath the Lord also said to a healed person, "Take up your bed and walk"; and he told the Pharisees that it was acceptable for the disciples to pick ears of corn and eat them on the Sabbath day (Matthew 12:1–9; Mark 2:23–28; Luke 6:1–6; John 5:9–19). In the spiritual meaning, these details all stand for being instructed in religious teachings.

The fact that the Sabbath day turned into a day for loving our neighbor is clear from the Lord's practice and teaching (Matthew 12:10–14; Mark 3:1–9; Luke 6:6–12; 13:10–18; 14:1–7; John 5:9–19; 7:22, 23; 9:14, 16).

All these passages make it clear why the Lord said that he was in fact the Lord of the Sabbath (Matthew 12:8; Mark 2:28; Luke 6:5). It follows from this saying of his that [before he came] the Sabbath day used to represent him.

302. In the *spiritual meaning*, this commandment refers to our being reformed and regenerated by the Lord. The *six days of labor* mean battling against the flesh and its cravings and also against the evils and falsities that are in us from hell. The *seventh day* means our becoming connected to the Lord and our being regenerated as a result. As long as this battle continues, we have spiritual labor; but when we have been regenerated, we rest. This will become clear from the points that will be made in the chapter on reformation and regeneration [*True Christianity* 571–625]—especially the following points that are discussed there: (1) *Regeneration progresses analogously to the way we are conceived, carried in the* womb, born, and brought up. (2) *The first phase in our being generated anew is called "reformation"; it has to do with our intellect. The second phase is called "regeneration"; it has to do with our will and then our intellect.* (3) *Our inner self has to be reformed first. Our outer self is then reformed through our inner self.* (4) *Then a battle develops between our inner and outer self. Whichever self wins, it will control the other.* (5) *When we have been regenerated, we have a new will and a new intellect.* And so on.

In the spiritual meaning, this commandment refers to our reformation and regeneration because these processes parallel the Lord's labors and battles against the hells, his victory over them, and then rest. The way he glorified his human manifestation and made it divine is the same way he reforms and regenerates us and makes us spiritual. This is what is meant by *following him.* The battles of the Lord are called labors, and were labors, as is clear from Isaiah 53 and 63. Similar things are called labors in us (Isaiah 65:23; Revelation 2:2, 3).

303. In the *heavenly meaning* this commandment refers to connecting to the Lord and having peace as a result, because we are then safe from hell. The *Sabbath* means rest, and in the highest sense peace. For this reason the Lord is called *the Prince of Peace,* and also calls himself peace. See the following passages:

> A Child is born to us; a Son is given to us. Authority will rest on his shoulder, and his name will be called Wonderful, Counselor, God, Hero, Father of Eternity, *Prince of Peace.* There will be no end to the increase of his government and peace. (Isaiah 9:6, 7)

> Jesus said, "*Peace* I leave to you. *My peace* I give to you." (John 14:27)

Jesus said, "I have spoken these things *so that you may have peace in me.*" (John 16:33)

How pleasant on the mountains are the feet of the One *proclaiming* and making us hear *peace,* saying, "Your king reigns." (Isaiah 52:7)

Jehovah will redeem my soul in peace. (Psalms 55:18)

The work of Jehovah is peace; the labor of justice is rest and safety forever so that they may live in a dwelling of peace, in tents of safety, and in tranquil rest. (Isaiah 32:17, 18)

Jesus said to the seventy whom he sent out,

Whatever home you come into, first say, *"The peace of the Lord,"* and if the people are *children of peace* then your *peace* will rest on them. (Luke 10:5, 6; Matthew 10:12, 13, 14)

Jehovah will speak *peace* to his people; *justice and peace* will kiss each other. (Psalms 85:8, 10)

When the Lord himself appeared to the disciples he said,

Peace to you. (John 20:19, 21, 26)

Isaiah 65 and 66 and other passages treat further the state of peace that people can come into with the Lord's help. The people to be accepted into the new church that the Lord is now establishing are going to come into this peace. (For the essence of the peace that the angels of heaven and those who are in the Lord have, see the work *Heaven and Hell* 284–290. These sections also make it clear why the Lord calls himself the Lord of the Sabbath, that is, the Lord of rest and peace.)

304. Heavenly peace is peace in relation to the hells—a peace because evils and falsities will not rise up from there and break in. Heavenly peace can be compared in many ways to earthly peace. For example, it can be compared to the peace

after wars when all are living in safety from their enemies, protected in their own city, in their house, with their own land and garden. It is as the prophet says, who speaks of heavenly peace in earthly language:

> They will each sit under their own vine and their own fig tree; no one will frighten them. (Micah 4:4; Isaiah 65:21, 22, 23)

Heavenly peace can be compared to rest and recreation for the mind after working extremely hard, or to a mother's consolation after giving birth, when her instinctive parental love unveils its pleasures. It can be compared to the serenity after storms, black clouds, and thunder; or to the spring that follows a severe winter, with the uplifting effect of seedlings in the fields and blossoms in the gardens, meadows, and woods; or to the state of mind felt by survivors of storms or hostilities at sea who reach port and set their feet on longed-for solid ground.

The Fourth Commandment
Honor Your Father and Your Mother So That Your Days Will Be Prolonged and It Will Be Well with You on Earth

305. This commandment reads this way in Exodus 20:12 and Deuteronomy 5:16. Honoring your father and your mother in the *earthly meaning*, which is the literal meaning, includes honoring our parents, obeying them, being devoted to them, and thanking them for the benefits they have given us—for feeding and clothing us, introducing us into the world so that we may become civil and moral people within it, and introducing us into heaven through religious instruction. In this way our parents have cared for our prosperity in time and our happiness to eternity. They do all these things from a love they have from the Lord, whose role they have played. In a comparable sense, it also means that wards whose parents have died are to honor their guardians.

In a broader sense, this commandment means honoring our monarch and government officials because on everyone's behalf they provide in a general way the necessities that parents provide in an individual way. In the broadest sense, this commandment means loving our country because it nurtures and protects us—it is called our "fatherland" from the word *father*. In fact, it is the parents themselves who need to give honor to the country and those who serve it, and to sow this habit in their children.

306. In the *spiritual meaning*, honoring your father and your mother refers to revering and loving God and the church. In this sense *father* means God—the Father of all—and *mother* means the church. In the heavens little children and angels know no other father or mother, since their rebirth in that world comes from the Lord through the church. This is why the Lord says, "Do not call anyone on earth your father, for your father is the One in the heavens" (Matthew 23:9). (These words apply to little children and angels in heaven, but not to little children and people on earth.) The Lord teaches something similar in the prayer that is shared by all Christian churches: "Our Father, who is in the heavens: your name must be kept holy."

In the spiritual meaning, *mother* stands for the church because as mothers on earth nourish their children with physical food, so the church nourishes people with spiritual food. For this reason in various places in the Word the church is called *mother*; for example, in Hosea: "Bring charges against your mother. She is not my wife and I am not her husband" (Hosea 2:2, 5). In Isaiah: "Where is the certificate of your mother's divorce, whom I put away?" (Isaiah 50:1; Ezekiel 16:45; 19:10). In the Gospels: "Jesus reached his hand toward the disciples and said, 'My mother and my brothers and sisters are those who hear the Word of God and do it'"

(Matthew 12:48, 49, 50; Mark 3:33, 34, 35; Luke 8:21; John 19:25, 26, 27).

307. In the *heavenly meaning, father* stands for our Lord Jesus Christ and *mother* stands for the communion of saints, meaning his church that is scattered throughout the entire world. The following passages show that the Lord is the *Father*:

A Child is born to us; a Son is given to us. His name will be called God, Hero, *Father of Eternity*, Prince of Peace. (Isaiah 9:6)

You are *our Father*. Abraham did not know us and Israel did not acknowledge us. *You are our Father*; our Redeemer from everlasting is your name. (Isaiah 63:16)

Philip said, "Show us the Father." Jesus says to him, "*Those who see me see the Father*. How then are you saying, 'Show us the Father'? Believe me that I am in the Father and the Father is in me." (John 14:7–11; 12:45)

The following passages show that in the heavenly meaning *mother* stands for the Lord's church:

I saw a city, the holy New Jerusalem, prepared as *a bride adorned for her husband*. (Revelation 21:2)

The angel said to John,

Come. I will show you *the bride, the wife of the Lamb*,

and he showed him the holy city Jerusalem (Revelation 21:9, 10).

The time for *the Lamb's wedding* has come; *his bride* has prepared herself. Blessed are those who are called to the *marriage supper of the Lamb*. (Revelation 19:7, 9; see also Matthew 9:15; Mark 2:19, 20; Luke 5:34, 35; John 3:29; 19:25, 26, 27)

The New Jerusalem means the new church that the Lord is establishing today (see *Revelation Unveiled* 880–881). This church, not the one before it, is the *wife* and *mother* in this sense. The spiritual offspring that are born from this marriage are acts of goodwill and true insights related to faith. The people who have these things from the Lord are called *the children of the wedding, children of God,* and *those who are born of him.*

308. An important idea to grasp is that a divine field of heavenly love constantly radiates from the Lord to all people who embrace the teaching of his church. Like little children in the world with their father and mother, these people obey the Lord, stay close to him, and want to be nourished, that is, instructed by him.

From this heavenly field an earthly field arises. It is a field of love for babies and children. It is absolutely universal. It affects not only people but also birds and animals, including even snakes. In fact, it affects not only animate things but also inanimate things. In order for the Lord to have an effect on inanimate things as he does on spiritual things, he created a sun that is like a father to the physical world and an earth that is like a mother to it. The marriage of the sun as a father and the earth as a mother produces all the growth that adorns the surface of the planet.

The influence of this heavenly field on the physical world occasions the miraculous progression in plants from seed to fruit to new seeds. It also results in many types of plant that turn their faces, so to speak, toward the sun by day and bow them when the sun sets, and in flowers that open when the sun rises and close when it sets. It also induces the songbirds to sing sweetly first thing in the morning and again after they have been fed by their mother, the earth. In these ways all these creatures honor their father and their mother.

All these phenomena are proof that through the sun and the earth the Lord makes available all the necessities for both the living beings and the inanimate things in the physical world. Therefore we read in David,

Praise Jehovah from the heavens. Praise him, sun and moon. Praise him from the earth, great sea creatures and the depths. Praise him, fruit trees and all cedars, the wild beast and every animal, creeping things and birds with wings, the kings of the earth and all peoples, young men and young women. (Psalms 147:7–12)

Also in Job:

Please, ask the animals and they will teach you. Ask the birds of heaven and they will make it known to you. Ask the shrub of the earth and it will instruct you. The fish in the sea will tell you the story. Which of all these things does not know that the hand of Jehovah has done this? (Job 12:7, 8, 9)

Ask and they will teach means watch, pay attention, and judge from these things that the Lord Jehovih created them.

The Fifth Commandment
You Are Not to Kill

309. This commandment, *You are not to kill,* in its *earthly meaning* means not killing people, inflicting on them any fatal wound, or mutilating their bodies. It also means not bringing any deadly evil against their names and reputations, since for many people their reputation and their life go hand in hand.

In a broader earthly meaning, murdering includes hostility, hatred, and revenge, which involve longing for someone's death. Murder lies hidden inside these feelings like an area that is still burning inside a piece of wood under the ashes. Hellfire is nothing else. This is why we say someone blazes with hatred or burns for revenge. These feelings are murders at the level of intent even if not in act. If fear of the law, retribution, or revenge were taken away, these feelings would burst into action, especially if the intent involved deception or savagery.

The following words of the Lord make it clear that hatred is murder:

You have heard that it was said by ancient people, "You are not to kill; and whoever kills will be exposed to judgment." But I say to you that any who are angry with their brother or sister for no good reason will be exposed to hellfire. (Matthew 5:21, 22)

The reason is that everything we intend is something we want and something we inwardly do.

310. In the *spiritual meaning*, murders stand for all methods of killing and destroying people's souls. There are many different methods, such as turning people away from God, religion, and divine worship; setting up roadblocks against such things; and persuading people to turn away from and even feel aversion to such things. All the devils and satans in hell practice these methods. People in our world who violate and prostitute the holy things of the church are connected to these devils and satans.

The king of the abyss, who is called Abaddon or Apollyon (meaning the Destroyer, Revelation 9:11), stands for people who use falsities to destroy souls. The *killed* in the prophetic Word have the same meaning, as for example in the following passages:

Jehovah God said, "Feed the sheep for slaughter whom their owners have killed." (Zechariah 11:4, 5, 7)

We have been killed all day long; we are considered a flock for slaughter. (Psalms 44:22)

He will cause those who are yet to come to take root in Jacob. Was he killed in the way that his henchmen would kill? (Isaiah 27:6, 7)

A stranger comes only in order to steal and slaughter the sheep. I have come so that they may have life and abundance.

(John 10:10; other such passages are Isaiah 14:21; 26:21; Ezekiel 37:9; Jeremiah 4:31; 12:3; Revelation 9:5; 11:7)

This is why the Devil is called "a murderer from the beginning" (John 8:44).

311. In the *heavenly meaning*, killing refers to being angry with the Lord for no good reason, hating him, and wanting to get rid of his name. People with such feelings are said to crucify the Lord; if he were to come back into the world again, they would do much the same thing the Jews did. This is the meaning of *the Lamb in a state as if killed* (Revelation 5:6; 13:8), and the meaning of *crucified* in Revelation 11:8; Hebrews 6:6; and Galatians 3:1.

312. Devils and satans in hell have made clear to me the inner quality of people who have not been reformed by the Lord. Devils and satans constantly have it in mind to kill the Lord. Because they cannot achieve this, they try to kill people who are devoted to the Lord. Since they cannot accomplish this the way people in the world could, they attack people with every effort to destroy their souls, that is, to demolish the faith and goodwill they have. The actual hatred and desire for revenge inside these devils look like fires that are dark and fires that are bright. Their hatreds look like dark fires and their desires for revenge look like bright fires. These feelings are not in fact fires, but they look like fires.

One can sometimes glimpse the savagery of the devils' hearts in visual form in the air above those devils. It looks as if they are battling, slaughtering, and massacring angels. Their feelings of anger and hatred against heaven are the source of these dreadful daydreams.

For another thing, these devils and satans look at a distance like wild animals of every kind—tigers, leopards, wolves, foxes, dogs, crocodiles, and snakes of all kinds. When devils and satans see tame animals in symbolic forms, they imagine themselves attacking the animals and trying to slaughter them.

I have seen devils that looked like dragons and were standing next to women with babies whom the dragons were trying to devour, like the situation we find in Revelation 12. These portrayals represent the devils' hatred against the Lord and his new church.

People in the world who want to destroy the Lord's church are similar to these devils and satans, although it does not seem that way to others who know these people, because their bodies—the instruments with which they practice moral actions—absorb their desires and keep them hidden. To the angels, however, who look at their spirits, not their bodies, these people look like the devils just mentioned. Who could ever realize things like this if the Lord had not opened someone's sight with the gift of looking into the spiritual world? Otherwise these points, along with many other things eminently worth knowing, would have remained forever hidden from the human race.

The Sixth Commandment
You Are Not to Commit Adultery

313. In its *earthly meaning*, this commandment covers not only committing adultery but also wanting to do and doing things that are obscene, and also having wanton thoughts and expressing them. As the Lord's words make clear, craving to commit adultery is committing adultery:

> You have heard that it was said by the ancients, "You are not to commit adultery." But I say to you that if a man looks at someone else's wife in such a way that he craves her, he has already committed adultery with her in his heart. (Matthew 5:27, 28)

The reason is that craving becomes a virtual deed when it is in the will. An attraction enters only our intellect, but an intention enters our will; and an intention based on a craving is a deed.

On these topics, see many things in the work *Marriage Love and Promiscuous Love*, published in Amsterdam, 1768. There are treatments there on the opposite of marriage love, §§423–443; on promiscuity, §§444[b]–460; on different kinds and degrees of adultery, §§478–499; on obsession with defloration, §§501–505; on the craving for variety, §§506–510; on the craving for rape, §§511, 512; on obsession with seducing the innocent, §§513, 514; and on accountability for the love of infidelity and the love of marriage, §§523–531. All the above are covered by this commandment in its earthly meaning.

314. In the s*piritual meaning, committing adultery* refers to contaminating the good things taught by the Word and falsifying its truths. The fact that *committing adultery* refers to these things has not yet been known, because the Word's spiritual meaning has been hidden until now. In the following passages it is obvious, however, that *committing adultery, being adulterous*, and *being promiscuous* have no other meaning in the Word:

> Run here and there through the streets of Jerusalem and see if you can find a man who *makes judgment and seeks truth*. When I fed them to the full, *they became promiscuous*. (Jeremiah 5:1, 7)

> Among the prophets of Jerusalem I have seen horrendous stubbornness, *committing adultery and walking in a lie*. (Jeremiah 23:14)

> They have acted foolishly in Israel. They have been *promiscuous, and have spoken my Word falsely*. (Jeremiah 29:23)

> They were *promiscuous* because they had abandoned Jehovah. (Hosea 4:10)

I will cut off the soul that looks off in the direction of sorcerers and soothsayers *to be promiscuous with them.* (Leviticus 20:6)

They are not to make a covenant with the inhabitants of the land; this is to prevent them from *being promiscuous with other gods.* (Exodus 34:15)

Because Babylon contaminates and falsifies the Word more than the rest do, it is called *the great whore,* and the following things are said of it in the book of Revelation:

Babylon has made all the nations drink the wine of the wrath of her promiscuity. (Revelation 14:8)

The angel said, "I will show you the judgment of the great whore with whom the kings of the earth were promiscuous." (Revelation 17:1, 2)

He judged the great whore who had corrupted the earth with her promiscuity. (Revelation 19:2)

Because the Jewish nation had falsified the Word, the Lord called it *an adulterous generation* (Matthew 12:39; 16:4; Mark 8:38) and *the seed of an adulterer* (Isaiah 57:3). There are also many other passages where adultery and promiscuity mean contamination and falsification of the Word; for example, Jeremiah 3:6, 8; 13:27; Ezekiel 16:15, 16, 26, 28, 29, 32, 33; 23:2, 3, 5, 7, 11, 14, 16, 17; Hosea 5:3; 6:10; Nahum 3:1, 3, 4.

315. In the *heavenly meaning, committing adultery* refers to denying the Word's holiness and desecrating the Word. This meaning follows from the spiritual meaning, which is contaminating the good things in the Word and falsifying its truths. People who in their heart laugh at everything having to do with the church and religion are people who deny the Word's holiness and desecrate the Word—in the Christian world every aspect of the church and religion comes from the Word.

316. People can seem chaste not only to others but even to themselves and yet be completely unchaste. There are various causes that produce this effect. People do not know that a sexual craving in their will is a deed, and it cannot be removed except by the Lord after they have practiced repentance. Abstaining from doing something does not make us chaste. What makes us chaste is abstaining from *wanting* to do something that we could in fact do, because doing it would be sinful.

For example, if a man abstains from adultery and promiscuity solely out of fear of civil law and its penalties; or out of fear that he will lose his reputation and respect; or out of fear of sexually transmitted disease; or out of fear of being harassed by his wife and having no peace at home; or out of a fear that the other woman's husband and relatives will avenge themselves on him, or that their servants will whip him; or out of miserliness; or out of lack of ability caused by disease, misuse, old age, or some other cause of impotence—in fact, if he abstains from adultery and promiscuity in obedience to any earthly or moral law but not at the same time to spiritual law, he nevertheless remains inwardly an adulterer and a promiscuous person. He still believes that adultery and promiscuity are not sins. In his spirit he does not make them unlawful before God. Therefore in his spirit he commits them, even if he does not commit them before the world in the flesh. As a result, when he becomes a spirit after death, he openly speaks in favor of such acts.

Adulterers could be compared to treaty breakers who violate agreements, or to the satyrs and priapuses of old who would wander in the woods and shout, "Where are virgins, brides, and wives to play with?" In fact, in the spiritual world, adulterers actually look like satyrs and priapuses. Adulterers could also be compared to goats that sniff for other goats, and dogs that run around in the streets looking and smelling for other dogs with which to have sex. And so on.

When adulterers get married, their sexual potency could be compared to the blooming of tulips in spring—in a month tulips lose their blossoms and wither away.

The Seventh Commandment
You Are Not to Steal

317. In the *earthly meaning*, this commandment literally covers not stealing, robbing, or privateering during a time of peace. It generally means not using stealth or pretense of any kind to take away someone else's possessions. It also covers all swindling, and illegal ways to profit, earn interest, and collect funds; also fraud in paying taxes and fees and in repaying loans.

Workers transgress against this commandment when they do their work dishonestly and deceptively; retailers, when they mislead customers with their merchandise, weighing, measuring, and calculations; officers, when they dip into their soldiers' pay; judges, when they tilt their judgments toward friends or relatives, or for bribes or other inducements, and thus bias their judgments or investigations and deprive others of goods that belong to those others by law.

318. In the *spiritual meaning, stealing* refers to using false and heretical ideas to deprive others of the truths of their faith. Priests are spiritual thieves if they minister only for financial benefit or status and they teach things that on the basis of the Word they see, or at least could see, are not true. They rob people of the means of salvation, which are the truths related to faith.

Priests like this are called *thieves* in the following passages in the Word:

Those who do not enter through the door to the sheepfold but climb up some other way are thieves and robbers. Thieves do not come in except to steal, slaughter, and destroy. (John 10:1, 10)

Store up treasures, not on earth but in heaven, where thieves do not come in and steal. (Matthew 6:19, 20)

If thieves, if people who knock things over in the night, come to you, how might you be cut off? Are they not going to steal whatever satisfies them? (Obadiah, verse 5)

They run here and there in the city, they run on the wall, they climb into houses, they come in through windows like a thief. (Joel 2:9)

They made a lie; the thief comes in, and the crowd scatters outside. (Hosea 7:1)

319. In the *heavenly meaning, thieves* stand for people who take divine power away from the Lord and people who claim the Lord's merit and justice for themselves. Even if these people worship God, they trust themselves, not him, and believe in themselves, not in him.

320. There are people who teach false and heretical things and convince the public that these things are true and theologically correct, and yet they read the Word and are therefore able to know what is false and what is true. There are also people who use errors to support false religious beliefs and lead people astray.

These people can be compared to con artists who perpetrate acts of fraud of every kind. Because the things just mentioned are actually thefts in a spiritual sense, these people can be compared to con artists who mint counterfeit coins, gild them or color them gold, and trade them as pure. They can also be compared to people who know skillful ways to cut and polish rock crystals, harden them, and sell them as diamonds. They can also be compared to people who would dress baboons and apes in human clothing with veils over their simian faces and lead them through town on horses or mules, claiming that they are nobles of an old and distinguished family.

They are also like people who would put masks covered in makeup over their own natural faces to hide their good looks. They are like people who would display selenite or mica, which gleam like gold and silver, and sell them as ore containing precious metals. They are like people who would put on theatrical performances to divert others from true divine worship and to lure those others away from church buildings to theaters.

People who support falsities of all kinds and care nothing for the truth, who play the part of priests solely for financial benefit or status and are therefore spiritual thieves, are like thieves who have master keys with which they can open the doors of any home. These people are also like leopards and eagles that look around with sharp eyes for areas that are rich in prey.

The Eighth Commandment
You Are Not to Bear False Witness against Your Neighbor

321. In its most accessible *earthly meaning*, [this commandment against] *bearing false witness against our neighbor* or testifying falsely includes not being a false witness before a judge, or before others outside of a courtroom, against someone who is wrongly accused of some evil. We are not to make such false assertions in the name of God or something sacred, or base them on our own authority or on some expertise for which we are well known.

In a broader earthly sense, this commandment applies to political lies and hypocrisies of every kind that have an evil intent, as well as disparagement and slander of our neighbors to undermine the status, name, and reputation on which their whole good character depends.

In the broadest earthly sense, this commandment includes plots, deceptions, and evil intent against anyone for a variety of motives such as hostility, hatred, desire for revenge, envy, rivalry, and so on. These evils have false witness hidden inside them.

322. In the *spiritual meaning*, testifying falsely refers to convincing people that a false belief is a true one and an evil life is a good one, and the reverse; but only if these things are done deliberately, not out of ignorance. Doing them deliberately is doing them after we know what truth and goodness are, not before. The Lord says, "If you were blind you would have no sin. But now that you say, 'We see,' your sin remains" (John 9:41).

This falseness is what is meant in the Word by *a lie* and this deliberateness is what is meant by *deceit* in the following passages:

> We are striking a pact with death; we are making an agreement with hell. We have put our trust in lying and have hidden ourselves with falsity. (Isaiah 28:15)

> They are a people of rebellion, lying children. They do not want to hear the law of Jehovah. (Isaiah 30:9)

> Everyone from prophet to priest is acting out a lie. (Jeremiah 8:10)

> The inhabitants speak a lie, and as for their tongue, deceit is in their mouths. (Micah 6:12)

> You are to destroy those who speak a lie. Jehovah loathes a man of deceit. (Psalms 5:6)

> They taught their tongue to tell a lie, to dwell in the midst of their deceit. (Jeremiah 9:5, 6)

Because *a lie* means a falsity, the Lord says, "The Devil speaks a lie from his own resources" (John 8:44). *A lie* also means falsity and deception in the following passages: Jeremiah

9:4; 23:14, 32; Ezekiel 13:15–19; 21:29; Hosea 7:1; 12:1; Nahum 3:1; Psalms 120:2, 3.

323. In the *heavenly meaning, testifying falsely* refers to blaspheming the Lord and the Word and driving the actual truth out of the church. The Lord is truth itself, and so is the Word. On the other hand, in this sense *testifying* means speaking the truth and *testimony* means the truth itself. This is why the Ten Commandments are called the *testimony* (Exodus 25:16, 21, 22; 31:7, 18; 32:15, 16; 40:20; Leviticus 16:13; Numbers 17:4, 10). Since the Lord is truth itself, he says that he testifies concerning himself. For the Lord as the truth itself, see John 14:6; Revelation 3:7, 14; for his testifying and being a witness to himself, see John 3:11; 8:13–19; 15:26; 18:37, 38.

324. There are people who say false, deliberately deceitful things and articulate them with a tone that emulates spiritual feeling. There are even some who cite truths from the Word as they do so, falsifying these truths in the process. The ancients had names for people like these: they called them magicians (see *Revelation Unveiled* 462) and also sorcerers, and snakes from the tree of the knowledge of good and evil.

These pretenders, liars, and deceivers are like people who talk in a pleasant and friendly way with their enemies, but while they are talking they have a dagger behind their back, ready to kill. They are like people who smear venom on their swords before attacking their enemies; or like people who put poison in a well and toxic substances in wine and pastries. They are like charming, attractive whores who carry a malignant sexually transmitted disease. They are like stinging plants that damage our olfactory nerves if we lift them to our noses to smell them. They are like sweetened poisons, or like dung dried out in the fall that gives off a pleasant aroma. In the Word they are described as leopards (see *Revelation Unveiled* 572).

The Ninth and Tenth Commandments

You Are Not to Covet Your Neighbor's Household; You Are Not to Covet Your Neighbor's Wife or His Servant or His Maid or His Ox or His Donkey or Anything That Is Your Neighbor's

325. In the catechism that is circulated these days, these have been divided into two commandments. One of them is the ninth commandment: *You are not to covet your neighbor's household.* The other is the tenth: *You are not to covet your neighbor's wife or his servant or his maid or his ox or his donkey or anything that is your neighbor's.* Because these two commandments are united and form just a single verse in Exodus 20:17 and in Deuteronomy 5:21, I have taken them up together. It is not my intention, however, to connect them into one commandment. I want to keep them distinguished into two commandments as they have been, since all the commandments are referred to as the *Ten Words* (Exodus 34:28; Deuteronomy 4:13; 10:4).

326. These two commandments look back to all the commandments that precede them. They teach and enjoin that we are not to do evil and that we are also not to crave doing evil. Therefore the Ten Commandments are not only for the outer self but also for the inner self. Someone who does not do evil things but nevertheless craves doing them is still doing them. The Lord says,

> If some man craves someone else's wife, he has already committed adultery with her in his heart. (Matthew 5:27, 28)

Our outer self does not become internal or become one with our inner self until our cravings have been removed. The Lord teaches this as well, when he says,

> Woe to you, scribes and Pharisees, because you clean the outside of your cup and plate, but the insides are full of plundering and self-indulgence. Blind Pharisee! First clean the

inside of your cup and plate, so that the outside may be clean
as well. (Matthew 23:25, 26)

The Lord says more on this in that whole chapter from beginning to end. The inner problems that are pharisaical are the
cravings to do what the first, second, fifth, sixth, seventh, and
eighth commandments say not to do.

It is generally known that while he was in the world, the
Lord gave the church inner teachings. The inner teachings for
the church tell us not to crave doing evil. He taught us this so
that our inner and outer self would become one, which is the
same as being born anew—something the Lord discussed
with Nicodemus (John 3). Only through the Lord can we be
born anew or regenerated, and therefore become inner people.

These two commandments look back to all the commandments that came before as things not to be coveted. Therefore
the household is mentioned first; then the wife; then the
servant, the maid, the ox, and the donkey; and finally everything that belongs to one's neighbor. The *household* comes
before everything on the rest of the list, for the husband, the
wife, the servant, the maid, the ox, and the donkey are all part
of it. The *wife*, who is mentioned next, comes before everything
on the rest of the list after that, for she is the woman in charge
of the household, as her husband is the man in charge of it.
The servant and the maid are under them, and the ox and the
donkey are under the servant and the maid. Finally, everything
below or beyond the servant and the maid is covered by the
phrase *anything that is your neighbor's*. This shows that generally and specifically, in both a broad and a narrow sense, these
two commandments look back to all the prior commandments.

327. In the *spiritual meaning*, these commandments prohibit
all the cravings that go against the spirit, that is, against the
spiritual qualities taught by the church, which primarily relate
to faith and goodwill. If our cravings were not tamed, our

flesh would pursue its own freedom and would quickly fall into every kind of wickedness. From Paul we know that "The flesh has cravings that go against the spirit and the spirit has cravings that go against the flesh" (Galatians 5:17). From James we know that "All are tested by their own craving. When they become captivated, then after the craving conceives, it gives birth to sin, and sin, when it reaches its final stage, brings forth death" (James 1:14, 15). From Peter we know that "The Lord holds for the judgment day the unjust who are to be punished, especially those who walk according to the flesh in craving" (2 Peter 2:9, 10).

In brief, these two commandments taken in their spiritual meaning look back to the spiritual meaning of all the commandments previously given, adding that we are not to crave doing those evil things. The same goes for all the commandments previously given in the heavenly meaning, but there is no point in listing them all again.

328. The cravings of the flesh—of the eyes and the other senses—when separated from the cravings of the spirit (meaning its feelings, desires, and pleasures) are identical to the cravings animals have. On their own, therefore, the cravings of the flesh are beastly. The desires of the spirit are what angels have; they are to be called desires that are truly human. Therefore the more we become addicted to the cravings of the flesh, the more of a beast and a wild animal we become; the more we give the desires of our spirit their due, the more of a human being and an angel we become.

The cravings of the flesh could be compared to grapes that have been parched and burnt or to wild grapes, while the desires of the spirit could be compared to juicy, flavorful grapes and to the taste of wine that has been pressed from them.

The cravings of the flesh are like stables that hold donkeys, goats, and pigs, while the desires of the spirit are like stables that hold thoroughbred horses, as well as sheep and lambs. In fact, the cravings of the flesh differ from the desires of the spirit the way a donkey differs from a horse, a goat from a sheep, and a pig from a lamb. They differ as much as slag and gold, lime and silver, coral and a ruby, and so on.

A craving and a deed are as closely connected as blood and flesh or oil and flame. The craving is in the deed the same way air from our lungs is in our breath and speech; or the wind is in the sail when we are sailing; or the water is in the waterwheel, causing the machinery to move and act.

The Ten Commandments Contain Everything about How to Love God and How to Love Our Neighbor

329. Eight of the commandments—the first, second, fifth, sixth, seventh, eighth, ninth, and tenth—say nothing about loving God or loving our neighbor. They do not say that we must love God or we must keep God's name holy. They do not say that we must love our neighbor, or deal honestly and uprightly with our neighbor. They say only, *There is to be no other God before my face; you are not to take God's name in vain; you are not to kill; you are not to commit adultery; you are not to steal; you are not to testify falsely; and you are not to covet what your neighbor has.* Briefly put, we are not to intend, think, or do evil against God or against our neighbor.

We are not commanded to do things that directly relate to goodwill; instead, we are commanded not to do things that are the opposite of goodwill. This is because the more we abstain from evils because they are sins, the more we want the goodness that relates to goodwill.

In loving God and our neighbor, the first step is not doing evil, and the second step is doing good, as you will see in the chapter on goodwill [*True Christianity* 435–438].

[2] There is a love of intending and doing good, and there is a love of intending and doing evil. These two loves are opposite to each other. The second is a hellish love and the first is a heavenly one. The entirety of hell loves doing evil and the entirety of heaven loves doing good.

We, the human race, have been born into evils of every kind. From birth onward we have tendencies toward things that come from hell. Unless we are born again or regenerated, we cannot come into heaven. Therefore the evil attributes we have from hell have to be removed first before we are able to want good attributes that come from heaven. None of us can be adopted by the Lord before we have been separated from the Devil. How our evil actions are removed and how we are brought to do good things will be shown in the chapter on repentance [*True Christianity* 509–570] and the chapter on reformation and regeneration [*True Christianity* 571–625].

[3] The Lord teaches in Isaiah that our evil actions have to be moved aside first before the good things we are doing become good before God:

> Wash yourselves; purify yourselves. Remove the evil of your actions from before my eyes. Learn to do what is good. Then, if your sins had been like scarlet, they will become as white as snow; if they had been red as crimson, they will be like wool. (Isaiah 1:16, 17, 18)

The following passage in Jeremiah is similar:

> Stand in the entrance to Jehovah's house and proclaim there this word. "Thus spoke Jehovah Sabaoth, the God of Israel: 'Make your ways and your works good. Do not put your trust in the words of a lie, saying, "The temple of Jehovah, the temple of Jehovah, the temple of Jehovah is here [that is, the church]." When you steal, kill, commit adultery, and swear falsely, then do you come and stand before me in this house that carries my name? Do you say, "We were carried away,"

when you are committing all these abominations? Has this house become a den of thieves? Behold I, even I, have seen it,' says Jehovah." (Jeremiah 7:2, 3, 4, 9, 10, 11)

[4] We are also taught by Isaiah that before we are washed or purified from evil, our prayers to God are not heard:

> Jehovah says, "Woe to a sinful nation, to a people heavy with wickedness. They have moved themselves backward. Therefore when you spread out your hands, I hide my eyes from you. Even if you increase your praying, I do not hear it." (Isaiah 1:4, 15)

When someone puts the Ten Commandments into action by abstaining from evil, goodwill is the result. This is clear from the Lord's own words in John:

> Jesus said, "The people who love me are those who have my commandments and follow them. Those who love me will be loved by my Father, and I will love them and manifest myself to them, and we will make a home with them." (John 14:21, 23)

The *commandments* mentioned here are specifically the Ten Commandments, which prescribe that we should not do, or crave to do, what is evil. If we do not do evil or crave to do evil, we love God and God loves us. This is the benefit we receive after something evil has been removed.

330. I have stated that the more we abstain from what is evil, the more we will and intend what is good, because evil and good are opposites. Evil comes from hell and good comes from heaven. Therefore the more hell—that is, evil— is removed, the closer we get to heaven and the more we focus on good.

The truth of this becomes obvious when we see eight of the Ten Commandments in this way. For example: (1) The less we worship other gods, the more we worship the true God.

(2) The less we take the name of God in vain, the more we love the things that come from God. (3) The less we want to kill and to act on the basis of hatred and revenge, the more we want what is good for our neighbor. (4) The less we want to commit adultery, the more we want to live faithfully with our spouse. (5) The less we want to steal, the more we aim to be honest. (6) The less we want to testify falsely, the more we want to think and speak what is true. (7) and (8) The less we covet what our neighbors have, the more we want our neighbors to be doing well with what they have. From this it becomes clear that the Ten Commandments contain everything about how to love God and our neighbor. Therefore Paul says,

> Those who love others have fulfilled the law. "You are not to commit adultery, you are not to kill, you are not to steal, you are not to be a false witness, you are not to covet things," and if anything else is commanded, it is included in this saying: "You are to love your neighbor as yourself." Goodwill does no evil to our neighbor. Therefore the fulfillment of the law is goodwill. (Romans 13:8, 9, 10)

To the above list, two principles need to be added that will benefit the new church: (1) On our own, none of us can abstain from evils because they are sins or do good things that are good before God. The more we abstain from evils because they are sins, the more we do good things from the Lord instead of from ourselves. (2) We need to abstain from evils and fight against them as if we were acting on our own. If we abstain from evils for any other reason than because they are sins, we are not abstaining from them, but merely making them invisible to the world.

331. Evil and good cannot coexist; the more evil is removed, the more good is focused on and felt. This is the case because all who are in the spiritual world have a field of their particular love emanating around them. This field spreads all around

and has an effect on others. It creates feelings of harmony or antipathy. These fields separate the good from the evil.

The fact that evil has to be removed before goodness is recognized, perceived, and loved could be compared with many situations that are possible in our world; for example, the following: Suppose someone keeps a leopard and a panther in an apartment and, as the one who feeds them, is able to live safely with them. No one else can visit unless their owner first removes these wild animals.

[2] Guests invited to the table of the king and queen would not forget to wash their faces and hands before attending. No bridegroom goes into the bedroom with his bride after the wedding without first washing himself all over and putting on a wedding garment. Anyone must first purify ore with fire and remove slag before getting pure gold or silver. Everyone separates the tares or weeds from the harvested wheat before taking it into the barn. Everyone removes the beards from harvested barley with threshing tools before bringing it home.

[3] Everyone cooks some of the juice out of raw meat before it becomes edible and is set on the table. Everyone knocks the grubs and caterpillars off the leaves of trees in the garden to prevent them from devouring the leaves and causing a loss of fruit. Everyone removes garbage from the house and the front entrance and cleans up those areas, especially when expecting a visit from a prince or the prince's daughter to whom one is engaged. Does any man love a young woman and propose to marry her if she is riddled with malignancies or covered all over with pustules and varicose veins, no matter how much she puts makeup on her face, wears gorgeous clothing, and makes an effort to be attractive by saying nice things and paying compliments?

[4] The need for us to purify ourselves from evils, and not to wait for the Lord to do it without our participation, is like a servant coming in with his face and clothes covered

in soot and dung, approaching his master, and saying, "Lord, wash me." Surely his master would tell him, "You foolish servant! What are you saying? Look, there is the water, the soap, and a towel. Don't you have hands? Don't they work? Wash yourself!"

The Lord God is going to say, "The means of being purified come from me. Your willingness and your power come from me. Therefore use these gifts and endowments of mine as your own and you will be purified." And so on.

The need for the outer self to be cleansed, but to be cleansed through the inner self, is something that the Lord teaches in Matthew chapter 23 from beginning to end.

—◆—

Biographical Note

≂

Emanuel Swedenborg (1688–1772) was born Emanuel Swedberg (or Svedberg) in Stockholm, Sweden, on January 29,
1688 (Julian calendar). He was the third of the nine children
of Jesper Swedberg (1653–1735) and Sara Behm (1666–1696).
At the age of eight he lost his mother. After the death of his
only older brother ten days later, he became the oldest living
son. In 1697 his father married Sara Bergia (1666–1720), who
developed great affection for Emanuel and left him a significant
inheritance. His father, a Lutheran clergyman, later became a
celebrated and controversial bishop, whose diocese included
the Swedish churches in Pennsylvania and in London, England.

After studying at the University of Uppsala (1699–1709),
Emanuel journeyed to England, the Netherlands, France, and
Germany (1710–1715) to study and work with leading scientists
in western Europe. Upon his return he apprenticed as an
engineer under the brilliant Swedish inventor Christopher
Polhem (1661–1751). He gained favor with Sweden's King
Charles XII (1682–1718), who gave him a salaried position as
an overseer of Sweden's mining industry (1716–1747). Although
Emanuel was engaged, he never married.

After the death of Charles XII, Emanuel was ennobled by
Queen Ulrika Eleonora (1688–1741), and his last name was

changed to Swedenborg (or Svedenborg). This change in status gave him a seat in the Swedish House of Nobles, where he remained an active participant in the Swedish government throughout his life.

A member of the Royal Swedish Academy of Sciences, he devoted himself to studies that culminated in a number of publications, most notably a comprehensive three-volume work on natural philosophy and metallurgy (1734) that brought him recognition across Europe as a scientist. After 1734 he redirected his research and publishing to a study of anatomy in search of the interface between the soul and body, making several significant discoveries in physiology.

From 1743 to 1745 he entered a transitional phase that resulted in a shift of his main focus from science to theology. Throughout the rest of his life he maintained that this shift was brought about by Jesus Christ, who appeared to him, called him to a new mission, and opened his perception to a permanent dual consciousness of this life and the life after death. He devoted the last decades of his life to studying Scripture and publishing eighteen theological titles that draw on the Bible, reasoning, and his own spiritual experiences. These works present a Christian theology with unique perspectives on the nature of God, the spiritual world, the Bible, the human mind, and the path to salvation.

Swedenborg died in London on March 29, 1772 (Gregorian calendar), at the age of eighty-four.

—◆—